The Meaning of Poems

Selected Poems (as) Poetics

James Berger

SPUYTEN DUYVIL

New York City

Poems selected from the following books: *Prior* (BlazeVox, 2013), *The OBU Manifestos* (Dispatches Editions/Spuyten Duyvil, 2017), *Under the Impression* (BlazeVox, 2020), *The OBU Manifestos, vol. 2* (Dispatches Editions/Spuyten Duyvil, 2020), *The Obvious Poems and the Worthless Poems* (Spuyten Duyvil, 2023), *I Once Met Kent Johnson* (Shuffaloff, 2023).

© 2024 James Berger
ISBN 978-1-963908-28-2

Library of Congress Control Number: 2024946222

Part 1: What is My Project?

What is my project, she asked	2
Word photons	4
Everyone has felt it	5
I've established that my poetry's principal quality	6
There is always some slim girl	8
My Father's Questions	11
Prior to Earth	13
Read and Unread	14

Part 2: Constraints

Afterwit, afterearth, trembling in in the buoyant	17
The Thing is an Obstacle	18
What it is, What it's Like, What it's Not	19
It Takes All Kinds, But it Doesn't Take Much	21
I Filled in My Form	22
will be code [this]	23
I Fell for the Bread Nurse	24

Part 3: Anthologies of Neglect

If I Only Knew	27
What's Dead on the Page	28
Time is Passing and I'm Not in the Groove	30
Someone Else Might Like This	31
Anthologies of Neglect	33
I could have turned a hundred times	37
OBU Interlude #5	39

Part 4: Fables

Prior to Water	43
Prior to Air	44
OBU Interlude #4	45
Is Your Mirror Up to the Task?	46
Spores	47

Part 5: Time-Ruin-Ratio

With Ratio/in Movement/ Subjective Correlative   51
Time in the Ruined House   59

Part 6: Par-Oidia: One Song Beside Another

The Art of the Future   67
Oh, That Story (for John Ashbery in a Bucket of Phonemes)   74

Part 7: Poetics/Politics

OBU Manifesto #39   83
Disintegrating Ode to a Senator   86
"and admit that the waters around you have grown…"   88
Addressing the Law   90
OBU Manifesto #1,988   92
I Once Met Kent Johnson   94

Part 8: Last Poems

The nut stops here. The child was there before   99
Manifesto # C#minor [approximately]   100
It has to be irregular   101
OBU Manifesto #42   102
What I think is nothing   104

Notes   107

Introduction

I'm not a poet-critic, unlike many of my friends and other poets I admire. I've been writing poems for a long time—call it fifty-five years or so. I've also been a scholar and teacher of literature for thirty years. But my scholarship and most of my teaching have not been about poetry. It's been more in the vein of modern fiction and cultural studies. I've written poetry, but I've never written *about* poetry. I've written no "criticism" and only a few reviews of poetry books. I've written no "poetics."

The reason for this absence has been partly my education through college and partly a certain obliviousness after college. The criticism I encountered as an undergrad (Columbia, class of '76) was largely still the New Criticism: "Tradition and the Individual Talent," the various "Fallacies," Empson's *Seven Types of Ambiguity*. The kids at Yale were already doing deconstruction with de Man and Hartman (and doing whatever it is one did with Bloom), but I knew nothing of that. We were still in the shadows of Trilling (*Sincerity and Authenticity* was hugely formative in my thinking) and Jacques Barzun. Very conservative. Soon after college, I discovered early Foucault and Derrida, having read reviews of some of their books in the *NY Times Book Review*. I discovered Kenneth Burke through my friend, the great and underread Diane Stevenson.

But also in college, I studied modern poetry and poetry writing with Kenneth Koch, and through Koch discovered O'Hara and Ashbery; and that set my poetic agenda for a number of years, such that getting *out* of that Koch/New York School influence was one of my principle tasks by my late 20's. I guess I never really did, entirely—but that is a good thing, I think. The struggles to free oneself of youthful influences; and then to grab hold of them and find what you really need are part of the process of becoming a poet who knows what he's doing (or is able to create an appropriate illusion of mature skill and then proceed as if he knew). And one notable feature of the New York poets of that first and of subsequence generations is that they did not write a lot of criticism of poetry (they did write a lot of art criticism), and they did not tend to spend much time thinking about "poetics." O'Hara wrote his "Personism Manifesto," from which I took away the marvelous thought that he wanted his poetic form to be like a pair of pants: loose enough to move in, but tight enough so that everyone would want to go to bed with him! Nuff said, right?! And Koch wrote his brilliant, funny, warm, and entirely a propos and useful poem, "The Art of Poetry." But the New York crowd were not poet-critics or theorists. That was a Black Mountain and West Coast thing: Olson, Duncan, Spicer thought and wrote about meta-poetry in ways that my teachers and guides in New York did not. So, I did not either... And at that time I wasn't reading Olson, Duncan, or Spicer.

The next generation–which really is also my generation or just a bit older or a bit younger–turned seriously to poetics and criticism. Nathaniel Mackey and Rachel Blau DuPlessis, Michael Davidon, Joseph Donahue, Norman Finkelstein, Mark Scroggins, Jeanne Heuving. Maria Damon, Patrick Pritchett, Michael Heller, Susan Schultz are all really good to great poets with some troves of criticism and poetics in their oeuvres. Oh, and what did I forget?! Seriously!? You know very well what I forgot: the L=A=N=G=U=A=G=E poets!!! Working out versions of poetics was absolutely at the center of that project, since it was in such large part, a conceptual project that required a meta-poetic discourse to bring it to full apprehension.

Of course, I missed them too. I encountered L=A=N=G=U=A=G=E in 1989, in a graduate seminar at the University of Virginia taught by Jerome McGann. Grad school was also when I read lots of social theory--Benjamin, Marcuse, Saussure, and Jameson, Foucault, Derrida, Baudrillard, Habermas, Rorty... all the people who were really useful to know as I read Bernstein, Hejinian, Silliman, Palmer and their comrades exploring the ideological inevitabilities of American language and the need for poetry to account for this core and residue, strip itself loose from subjectivity, beauty, syntax, semantics, grammar and every conceivable zone where capitalist ideology might cache and secrete itself. What fun! But I never really bought it. I preferred the theory to the poetry–the theory, to my ears, contained more poetry.

L=A=N=G=U=A=G=E was exciting, but I didn't want to do what they were doing. They taught me new possibilities of disjunction and, what can I call it–depersonification, using other voices that were not me, or trying to get outside the whole idea of voice. Hejinian was my favorite of the L-gang, the most Wordsworthian poet of the movement. Only a dozen or so years later, I discovered Rachel Blau DuPlessis–is she, was she, a L=A=N=G=U=A=G=E poet? No? Yes? Does it matter? No, actually, not at all.

And so, having immersed myself in L=A=N=G=U=A=G=E for a short spell, I determined that I really and truly did not need to explicitly theorize my poetry or any poetry. I worked at writing better poems and I worked at my career as an academic scholar and teacher. And my scholarly work did, in fact, grow from, around, and back toward my work and play in poetry. My book, on post-apocalyptic thinking (*After the End*), and my book on language and cognitive impairment in literature (*The Disarticulate*) both shaped intellectual encounters with the imagined limits of language, with catachresis, the boundaries of what was thinkable and utterable. But still, in the actual act of writing, in the expenditure of time, the scholarship was in one place, the poetry in another.

Then, just about a year and a half ago–or some time after 2020–I began to think differently. I began to think, ok, why *don't* I write anything about poetry? I've been writing poetry all these years. Why don't I have some concept of a poetics? On the one hand, all that's necessary is the poems. That's what I always believed. But through all these years of writing, do I really have no ideas about what I've been doing? Have I simply been some Aeolian chime reverberating perception and feeling, experience in life and in poetic form... and there we are! The Naive Poet. Well, no; no, that seems implausible. I also *think*, for better or worse. Over the past decade, I'd met and gotten to know in varying capacities a number of poet-critic types: Mark Scroggins, Norman Finkelstein, Rachel Blau DuPlessis, Susan Schultz. I liked a lot of what they were doing. But I also didn't think I could do quite the things that they were doing. I still did not want to do scholarly research about poetry. And I didn't want to write what might be considered "criticism." Rachel was clearly doing something different with those astonishing mixed-genre essays in *The Pink Guitar*. That seemed a direction, if I could figure out how to do it.

Another influence in my shift was getting to know Kent Johnson as we worked together in putting together and publishing *The OBU Manifestos* after the election of Trump in 2016. I read a lot in Kent and Mike Boughn's online journal, *Dispatches from the Poetry Wars*, where a lot of fundamental questions about poetry were consistently asked in fundamental ways. What is it for? What are we doing? How really can we understand the politics of poetry? How do we understand the histories of poetry and how do we place ourselves within and against them? It was a journal of good questions. Writing *OBU* (the manifestos of the movement that does not exist), corresponding with Kent, reading *Dispatches* all moved me in ways I didn't necessarily perceive toward something resembling a poetics.

Finally, though, what I wanted to know, and to figure out a way to investigate, was a most basic question: how do I encounter a poem? What species of directness and what paths of mediation converge, diverge, reverge to make the act of reading? How can I articulate my relation to a poem? How does my experience and identification as a poet myself affect my reading of poems? I found myself re-reading Schiller's famous, brilliant, weird, impossible essay, "On Naive and Sentimental Poetry"; and I thought, what might it be to concoct a "Naive and Sentimental Poetics"?! And I set about trying to approach books of poems as if... I had never read a poem, did not know what a poem was, did not know anything of the history of poetry. As in Williams' great poem in *Spring and All*, I would "enter the new world naked, cold, uncertain of all save that [I] enter." There it would be–the Naive poetics; something like the New Criticism close reading, but far far more elemental. It would be a Rousseauian reading–poetry in a state of nature, and really the opposite of the hyper-sophistication of L=A=N=G=U=A=G=E. But, of course, such an attitude is impossible. One is always clothed in some garment or other. A reader can never be naked. We bring what we bring and can never quite achieve the desired disrobing. Our reading, like our writing, is, in Schiller's terms, "sentimental," which is to say, self-aware, not naked, not innocent. All reading and writing oscillate between these postures, trying to achieve the one, falling back toward the other.

So, I started doing those readings and writing "On Naive and Sentimental Poetics," and I'm still working at it.

But then something else occurred to me. I had thought that I had never written any sort of poetics, but I realized I was mistaken. I had been writing a great deal of poetics. As I looked back at the poetry I'd been writing and then publishing throughout my life as a poet, I saw that a surprising number of my poems were in some regard about poetry–about their own composition, about composition in general, about form, about poetic projects, about how experience is translated/carried across into language, sometimes expressed as metaphor or allegory, sometimes as autobiographical anecdote, sometimes with explicit focus, sometimes as casual reference. Over the years, it appeared that I had engaged in an ongoing poetics after all. And, since it was a poetics within poems themselves, a poetry as poetics, it is not, in effect, a theory. It is poetics in action, poetics on the fly. If it is knowledge (and here I borrow from Jonathan Kramnick's recent book, *Criticism and Truth: On Method in Literary Studies*), this poetics in poetry expresses a knowing *how* rather than a knowing *that*. It does not expound or explain. It shows what it says through being what it is. It acts out the process of meaning what it says–which is, as I see it, all that poetry can mean.

So, I put together a Selected Poems–selected not on the basis of quality (though I think and hope these are among my better poems and are good ones regardless) and not organized according to chronology, but selected as poems that express or enact ideas and practices of poetry; poems that work toward articulating a poetics.

The poems are not examples of "ars poetica." They convey no general principles of poetry. "A poem should not mean/But be." But there, he said it, what it *should* do. Or the "imaginary gardens with real toads in them..." and

> "the raw material of poetry in
>   all its rawness, and
>   that which is on the other hand,
>   genuine..."

Right, but there, she *said* it, "the raw material" the "genuine." How can that be genuine? That's *ars poetica*, not poetry, and not poetry-as-poetics. And that's by a great poet, and it's not a bad poem though not one of her best. Or there's Koch, whose "Art of Poetry" is the best of that genre I know of. It's about the actual activity of writing poems and about the life that a poet might live when he's not writing poems, and it's moving and funny.

And many poets have written something like poems-as-poetics poems. All the poet-critics I mentioned have written them. Probably most poets conceive of them at one point or other--trying to account for poetic practice as one is practicing.

The book's title, *The Meaning of Poems*, is taken from Walt Whitman, from "Song of Myself" section 2:

> Have you reckon'd a thousand acres much? have you reckon'd the earth much?
> Have you practis'd so long to learn to read?
> Have you felt so proud to get at the meaning of poems?
> Stop this day and night with me and you shall possess the origin of all poems,
> You shall possess the good of the earth and sun, (there are millions of suns left,)
> You shall no longer take things at second or third hand, nor look through the eyes of the dead, nor feed on the spectres in books,
> You shall not look through my eyes either, nor take things from me,
> You shall listen to all sides and filter them from your self.

A wonderful formulation of Schiller's opposition–the dream of immediacy; but an immediacy somehow available through the act of reading a poem! My poems are not like this one, sadly. There is no poem like this one. And how in truth do you get to "the meaning of poems"? What does that even mean?

My motto in this work of poetics that I've embarked on: *What does a poem mean? It means what it says.* Frank Stella said something similar about his paintings. "What you see is what you see." Something of a poetics there. Poetics while standing on one foot, for those who get that allusion.

PART 1

What's My Project?

What is my project, she asked.
        Am I just writing poems,
                or do I have a project?

What can I answer?
                      Only to enter the dead tradition
                      plant my spurs in the dead horse's flanks.

                      My project is to slog
                      my mortality in the dried vein

                      of lyric, and to claim
                      at last my incapacity

                      as my own.
                                  I note that others

      still concoct these little mechanisms
            with their highlights of figured pain
                                  vivid backsplash
                                that draws together
                      the well-designed verbal kitchen.

And everything is well-designed nowadays, you can't deny that.
The training is impeccable. Every serious college jazz player
can fly through the changes on "Giant Steps," probably transpose
them through all twelve keys, why not?
                              And every trained poet can soar with sober joy
                                  through the repertoire of self and world
                                        and paradox and sound
                                              and image and allusion
                and it's all good. The general technical standard
                has never been higher.
Look at all the great design shows on TV.
                          You could easily have poetry makeovers.
Bring in your old dull poem you just don't know what to do with
                    and the attractive young poem design team will innovate
                          with a dash of tradition, knock out
                                  some stanza walls
bring out the underlying forms and
                make for you a poem
                      that's both really you
                                    and who you want to be!

Word-photons
shoot up against some object;
words stick to it and *there* it is,
there and then and never again
exactly that, never again
necessary, in that present way.

A white placard beneath it contains
its curses and proscriptions.

Everyone has felt it,
electricity of the fingers,
the merger of eyes into face--
not death,
just the shedding of context:
the inhalation exhaled
as "lyric."

I've established that my poetry's
                              principal quality
                                                  is evasion.
I've always thought that I was
                              exploring the edges of language,
the place where language meets
                              not-language–
                                                  sensation, neurology:
the unsayable, not just as trauma
                              or the sublime or the sacred
but as experience
                in all regards

                                          all untranslatable,
                                                a massive bundle unable
                          to be carried across intact
                                that boundary not a boundary–
                                            uncontiguous, not on the same plane.

Or such was my theory.
                      And of course it *has*
                                    occurred to me
that my most deeply
                defining experience of language
                                        was the fact
of my two sisters' inability to speak–
                            their mental retardation,
                                            as we used to call it

It has occurred to me
that my sisters are almost entirely
missing from my poetry--

like a great centripetal shove,
as if an orchestral composition
explicitly calls for a certain instrument,
say a somewhat unusual one,
maybe a euphonium,
and then for the entire piece
marks it "*tacit.*"

There is always some slim girl,
                      dark hair, very serious,
                                      on a bicycle even in cold weather–

She could be my sister, unaging
                      as my real sisters
                                  fail to age

(they seem gradually just
                    to wear down over time).
                                  The girl is always bicycling

always impossibly
                pretty, on another plane,
                            in another life.

If she were here she could comfort me–
but then it would be *me*
in another life, her life, her brother.
It would be me who stayed in Boston
instead of coming to NY,
studied with Levertov instead of Koch,
married younger, had a child, divorced,
moved toward a different aesthetic.
I had friends who were poets,
we encouraged each other, I gave readings,
got a book together on a small press,
never went to grad school, didn't go
to Tanzania, never met Jennifer, obviously,
achieved a minor career, not too bad.

My second marriage made me happy,
        I stayed close to my son from my first marriage–
            had another child, another son; two boys.
And my sister's bicycle and her serious face
                      were absent from all my poems.

I published another book.
        The natural world enchanted me.
        I learned to play the mandolin,
 never got back to the brass instruments,
        never started playing jazz.
            I put a piece in <u>Ploughshares</u>
and one in <u>Prairie Schooner</u>.
        I worked hard at my craft.
            I wanted to capture the beauty of moments.

My family and I did a lot of hiking in western Mass.

I could identify plants, I put a little time
into that, seemed like a good thing to do,
to name what I saw and loved.
I decided not to take up fishing.

I taught children with special needs,
eventually I administered the program.
I wrote a book of poems about those experiences
and it was well received.

My sister and her beautiful serious face.

My Father's Questions

He was a man of questions–
big ones and small ones, smart and stupid, annoying questions,
repetitive, essential, obvious.
He always would ask me if I had friends,
did I have a social life, whom did I see and spend time with?
(And sure, I saw people, I had colleagues,
my tennis friends, my music friends,
poetry friends, politics friends;
then there were the parents-of-my-children's-friends
friends. But did I have *friends*?).
Why did he always ask me that question?

And he asks me, how is my marriage?
Are we working on it? Are we in therapy?
He asks me, what am I teaching? Will I send him a syllabus?
He asks me, when I give a poetry reading, do I explain
the poems, do I give any kind of introduction or context?
Because I really ought to, they're not very easy to understand.
Do I read the poems in *The New Yorker*? Mine are a lot like those,
he says, very obscure, very self-involved.
(And I say, no, my poems are not at all like the poems in *The New Yorker*;
those poems are boring, mine are entertaining).

He asks me, when I teach my classes, do I ever get the students
to think about what makes a work of literature *great*?
He asks me, why don't I write a paper
on why literary styles change from one historical period to another?
He asks me, has anyone ever done that?
He asks me, have you ever thought of teaching a course
on why literature is important?
He asks me, do I ever think about what it means to be alive
or what life means, why are we here, what's our purpose?
And I say, Jesus Christ, Dad, how the fuck should I know? I mean,
of course, all of the above, what the hell?!

But maybe I don't. Maybe I ask those questions the same way I have friendships,
not in truth, only instrumentally.

felt–that was a plow–until
flesh seared–
then breathing reached–its
temperature–utmost–
beyond a roar.
No public thought–
or contemplation–touched–
none at all–

Prior to Earth

the other species contributed
the excavation took shape
a mound was formed beside the ditch
and we pulled from the ditch
an enormous wooden frame
we said, was it you,
was it your people?
The frame was caked in dirt
we could see indentations,
were there jewels there
had it been connected to some machinery?

Read and unread

(through reeds).
Red/Unred.
Some colors are signals
some design--
patterns enunce port-
end partic-
ulate general
pointings.
There is price
between inter and
predation,
accost to redeem
what means?
Can you interpret for me?
The meaning will not be
what you intend
or send
or what I receive
and configure--
Is there nothing precise here?
What's carried
over sent across thrown
forward
bounced back?
There is nothing precise here.
It's all unred, about to be red,
but for the blue note
tagging the last syllable
and the green fruit
you should not eat
yet.

PART 2
Constraints

Afterwit, afterearth, trembling in the buoyant–
I silence myself so I can listen;
bending, unbending, my words fasten
to you, myself again, regressing, unsilent.
Undershod, understolen, traipsing with soil and
bustling in crisis to shred and loosen
you from me so I can hear you, so this glisten
on your hand is not me, not reliant
on my wish to be you. I beg
you to go to another room, exchange your tongue,
adopt a language I can never translate.
Then, cacaphonous, we can embrace, yet not renege
our separation, that draft of half a wing--
after, under–daft fluttering of sudden, dazzling weight.

The thing is an obstacle

like fallen trees.

They stop a road, but not a path.

On the path, you bend down and slide under one

then jump or hoist yourself over the next

and you get by.

In a car, you can do nothing.

Turn around. Wait for the road crew.

The obstacle, as if it had a mind,

selects your adroitness; if you can't do it,

you wouldn't be on the path. If

you're there, you can do it.

Why should there not be a fallen tree on the path?

The road's premise is lack of obstacle.

The car has no adroitness.

What it is, what it's like, what it's not

It isn't optimal, it isn't corpulent, it isn't vestigial
It isn't crapulous, it isn't verdant, it isn't cancerous
It isn't parodic, it isn't opulent, it isn't like a bird
It isn't optical, it isn't reciprocal, it isn't pendant
It isn't pending, it isn't fractal bending, it isn't shodden hoglike
It isn't wending, it isn't shedding, it isn't wedding
It isn't lucent, it isn't sending, it isn't optimal
It isn't reluctant, it isn't calculated, it isn't wise
It isn't wizened, it isn't frazzled, it isn't dazzled,
It isn't like a word

Is it possible that accidental leanings produce meanings
or accidental loopings produce groupings or accidental blendings
mendings, do accidental liftings produce shiftings, do accidental
parkings produce markings, do accidental seemings
produce gleamings, but do accidental recalcitrances produce dances,
do accidents produce new accidents, or are they precedents?

Do accidental precedents produce testimonies?
Is every precedent an accident?
Is every act a fact, is every neglect an effect

It isn't a fact, it isn't an act, it isn't intact
it isn't cracked, it isn't checked, it isn't wrecked
Is isn't shielding we're wielding, it isn't melting you're shearing
It isn't from grimness to dimness, it isn't collage
It isn't preference, it isn't reference, it isn't deference
It isn't physics, it isn't neuroscience, it isn't genetics
It isn't history, it isn't law, it isn't culture
It isn't *Tuche*, it isn't *Ananche*, it isn't Beyoncé
It isn't the Fall, it isn't the Wall, it isn't the Call

Is it possible that purposeful tics suppose bricks?
Could it be automatic, or could there be destiny in the sudden expansion?
Do wells reveal fissures reveal ores reveal cores reveal the primal weave
       reveal apostrophe reveal prosopopoeia?

Is it improvisation or is it error?
A kind of swivel?
What is the real nature of a conjunction?
Do suppressed sluices mimic voices?

It Takes All Kinds, But It Doesn't Take Much...

Well it takes all kinds, does it not? Indeed, it takes all kinds.
There is no kind of a kind that it doesn't take. It takes it.
It takes them. Not the entirety of the kind, but at the least
one of a kind; of each kind. Because, as has been mentioned,
it takes *all* kinds. With that in mind, would you be so kind
as to respond in kind. And yet, what is meant, precisely,
by this rind, for clearly we are not made privy to what has
been innerly designed. We see what might unwind
from somewhere behind, or around, or somewhere
in the general vicinity, but if in fact it takes, as we assert,
all kinds, on what grounds do we determine if a given specimen
is of a kind, is one of that kind (which is not to say or to imply
the one of that kind), or is merely the kin
of the kind, or a copy of the kind, a projection of the mind
of another kind. Or, conversely, more generously, should we say
that "kind" is what appears as kind; that kind is kin
or kind is rind, or kind is what you find, around
or behind. Or, what you lose in exactitude,
you gain in kindness? So, if kindness would unwind,
would it be lessened, flattened, diminished in thickness?
What would then be distinguishable? If there were to be
generalized kindness, how could we tell one kind from another?
Are you our sister, our brother? Or, as the baby bird
asked the backhoe, Are you my mother?
But why not? There is precedent, it appears, for all
kinship. If someone dances, who is to say
they don't dance well? What kind of dance?
To strain for rhyme, let's call it "ecumenical."
So, that's the kind it takes?
That buzzing puts me to sleep, but I can't sleep.
I'm in Plentitude! But one kind pokes
while the other prods.

I Filled in My Form

I filled in my form and bubbles scattered in a brilliant display,
but I had already read it.

A young poet called it the "Yandiflit"--
where each letter exuded a membrane

hungry to repeat itself before it burst.
It was a joyful form.

The bubbles knew that their integrities were momentary.
I opened my mouth to the rising maelstroms.

Objects can be forms of laughter.

Children hide toys in the deep piles of leaves.

Could there be no pressure?

The muttering elevator, the garage of grain–

If the problem of scale could be determined

I myself could fit onto a postage stamp.

So: poetry is linked to knowledge.
So: resist normativity.
So: poetry is really not experimental.
So: what would it mean for poetry to be
        a privileged form of knowledge?

Great questions for the panel!

will be code [this]
space between obstacles

forecast to project [all]
wind and varies

end of one world [and]
vacancy origins

code paper [recognition]
dismantling cogs

Did you say "illusion" or "elusive"?
Nothing between nerves [asphalt]

I said the distinction was *illusive*
careful [abundance]

quick retrieval [permanent]
Which do you recognize?

Dismantle distinguish [demeanor]
brusque abundance of demeanors

The cog was permanent
its emotion was

I Fell for the Bread Nurse

I fell for the Bread Nurse,
inert, motionless;
I felt I could not rise
until she kneaded me.
Along the shelves she walked,
healing and nourishing.
I disassemble
my rigid theater
and the tics
that colonize
my extremities.
When the Bread Nurse smiles,
no architecture
of ligaments can hold
its cantilever.

I fell for
         the Bread Nurse

I fell
     in pixilated wounds

I fell
     in round excessive fermenting

         The room is yeasted

The Bread Nurse formed me

then she baked me.

I rise in joy

through the oven's orthodoxy.

PART 3
Anthologies of Neglect

If I Only Knew

If I only knew what I thought I knew...
And I thought I knew--not everything; of course,
not that, I wasn't that dumb–but a substantial amount,
a chunk that put me in a solid place
as far as knowing was concerned.
But I didn't know the world was so big.
I thought it was really much smaller.
I didn't know that each place I thought completed
was just a small plot of a far-extending work-in-progress
that was itself part of countless interchanges,
and there I was nibbling on a small peninsula
that would barely have registered
on the most tentative map of that terrain.
But if I'd known, if I'd devoted myself to knowing,
and if I'd known *how* to know,
if the resonance had been revealed to me,
if I'd known whom to know,
if I'd known how to inhabit,
if I'd just known how to say to someone,
"Show me how, show me what I need to know..."
Or if I'd known how to let go of the shyness and arrogance
that prevented me from asking
and from knowing,
then I would have seen that my grand belief horizon
was a pile of sticks, a barricade
of assumptions assembled in fear and impatience.
But I didn't know.
In consequence,
I thought I could do anything.

What's Dead on the Page

What's dead on the page is dead on the page.
Whatever generates it dead on the page is dead on the page.
One oops two ps one-to-tive hinge probability
what is *arranged* as such is in a bloody parcel and famous
historical dead people suffer lunch around themselves
to filch and be filched of offer numerical potencies.
Always or in general mist of intangible portentous.
Don't blame the subject this is not subjective.
Imperatives derives from a prior organization internal
subject of course to standard defective outcome.
What were the previous or historical imperatives derived?
Cutting the edge poor edge.
Mirrors are mist obscurity wears paint.

Now back to weaning we're suffering milk
writing is algorithm writing is removing a hinge
Oh the looseness of the slippage between parallel
and ambient I can't choose what to repeat I
can feel at every moment a process I reject.
Introduce a topic again imperative this is my podcast.
Such feeling such decision such orbit such jettison.
Every hive gets whacked. Never be twice.

Why is this poem always telling someone what to do?
Imperative to swerve arms shot out and falling.
Why at every does? Why when a pivot signals?
Ginger is good for digestion. Chamomile for nerves.
I keep pretending that someone can do it for me.
I look at the computer and say, you know more than I do,
you have a system, if y then y, if x then not x, if noun-predicate
then adjective conjunction then decision tree optional
semantic lift up from syntax, if referent then sliding,
if door then breeze if known name then say if need
say more say more confess to mourning lie abject

in a mountain phased from common political
but tells nothing, nothing really, portent,
annunciation you can do nothing but receive
the poem opens its womb and the small named figure
dead on the page is circumvalent
I will give no name you must choose a name
choose a name

Time is Passing and I'm not in the Groove

There is the aging
of the universe and
there is the universal

aging.
There is the time it takes
to decide

to move and the delay
between then
and the beat.

I'm bad... imprecise in the "&,"
never finding the "1";
someone tells me every two bars

the cymbal will hit it,
so listen:
find the latch, get the key,

be in the pocket.
But I can't hear the time--
I think oracular, play static.

Someone Else Might Like This

Someone else might like this; I don't. I don't think it has any imagery
or discernable form or implicit form, its word choices
are pedestrian, that means at a slow walk across a crowded street
and you don't get to see the street or the crowd, which are the interesting parts,
there's no interesting intellectual or moral tension, I mean no tug
that puts a reader in a slightly uncomfortable place which is
nonetheless pleasing because he or she recognizes there's something
important and real in the indecisiveness he's forced to reenact;
which is to say, the poem lacks verisimilitude, and it falls into the venerable
category of "who gives a fuck?"--
There are too many words and not enough of the right ones,
so the editor tries to cut, and cut, and then you're left with, pretty much,
not a whole lot, a lot of not much; which is not to say it's worthless,
you keep thinking there *was* an impulse worth putting out there
and now worth preserving, if it's possible– like a tune you're trying to put words to,
and you're Rogers, you've got the tune, and somewhere out there is Hart,
you'd even settle for Hammerstein, but *someone*, clearly it's not you,
someone can add some lyrics, then you look again at the score,
and there's no tune at all there, it's more like a baseball box score
and you see all these guys, how many times they were at bat, how many hits,
runs, walks, strikeouts, rbi's, and the various pitchers' lines, and with a small effort
you can reconstruct the game, a fair amount of it, not like a whole scorecard
like you might do if you were there, but it's a lot of data,
it's a deep notation, if you love the game it's a powerful aesthetic.
Its application penetrates the mind; and if you read it at all, it's already in the heart.
But it lacks a presence in the muscles, that's the real jump, that's the place
the poem would begin, if a poem could fit there. If a poem could fit there,
it would speak from the muscles. The song's lyrics are only actual when sung,
when they vibrate. Is this true? I'm wondering not how to give the poem
an image, but how to give it a muscle, a larynx and a tympanum.
Conrad said, "above all, to make you *see*"; no– not even true for him.
The point is to make you move. The ball is thrown, it spins, a batter swings,
 the ball is hit (let's say) to right field, the runner from first rounds second, accelerates,
and everything shifts, fields and trajectories reorient themselves and within the form,

the boundaries, a different set of shapes and relationships are aligned
as if kaleidoscopically, but with purpose, a set of purposes, coordinated
and in opposition, achieved through rapid, muscular thought.
Sounds very macho… Yes? No? Are "rapid" and "muscular" masculine terms?
Is "thought" a masculine term? In whose view? I don't think they should be,
but how about "kinesthetic," the feeling of movement, sense of one's own body,
by extension (via mirror neurons?) of bodies, moving, in general.
The poem is the body moving. Except it's not. The body dancing.
The body thinking. The body in infinite regression to the body,
to the body, to the organic material to the inorganic material
to the immaterial, which is most material. Let's assume:
the horse and the coachman in that "bed of compassion"; Stevie sees it,
you see it; you see how it becomes visible, then you see how it falls
apart having "the only one disadvantage of being difficult of application
on a large scale." And that's the kicker, that's when you know–you don't see,
you're on surer, more terrible ground–that what you see isn't what matters.
It's necessary that you see it, but only because of where it fits
with the entire system, that you can never see,
that has to be the object of your knowledge, and yet there's not an algorithm either,
no set of quantifiable variables that will give you the representation
you need to judge it. You're in it, you're of it, you're grasping
at every detail as if a synecdoche were a life raft.

"The Anthologies of Neglect"

What do they show? What do they prove?
I don't know...
That lots of people can write well and have something to say;
that the poets that people know, have read, or even just have heard of,
are not so much better, if at all, than the poets, in far greater numbers,
that people have never heard of, who published little
or who published a fair amount but it was soon forgotten,
what little of it was read at all, ever, by anyone.
And one can say, this is hopeful and encouraging–
that talent and commitment are so common, that poetry
is a common and fluid medium and so many speak it;
it's not isolated, isolating, elite, prodigious, hermetic...
Whatever is commonest, nearest, cheapest, easiest is me, wrote Walt,
        and we see that it's true.
Perhaps not everyone can write well, I mean really well,
but far more people than we might think.
"Genius," whatever that is, is not the prerequisite.
Determination and persistence and enough occasional inspiration
to make the activity enjoyable enough to keep at it–
That sense that, just once in a while, you think, Yeah, I nailed it!
these are the qualities required.
Oh, and you have to love poetry, the thing and history that it is,
however you think of it.
But it's also depressing and dispiriting, this plethora of neglected talent.
To think that so much depends on luck and circumstance, on one's social skills,
charm, loquaciousness, or some aura of mystery, or certain
signals of obvious brilliance, or just a bit of sycophancy, or the sullen outsider/outlaw stance,
or accessibility of one's work to academic trends, or being really good-looking,
or convincing at least one small group of writers with some influence
that you are a person producing work that must be attended to,
and they promote it,
and you yourself sure as hell promote it–
or, who knows what? Who knows?
And it's depressing to think that poetic acclaim

is pretty much just another niche market of the larger
culture of celebrity.
Luck, circumstance, and marketing... and good writing, of course.
But we've now established that the recipients of fame or notice
(as least in the small ways that poets dole it out)
differ little in terms of the quality of their work
from the recipients of neglect.
The "Great Poets of Our Time"–it's not a list of five, or twenty,
it's a list of three hundred, or five hundred!
And our anthology must be a rotating anthology,
each year it will be different, and in a different medium.
Each year a different collective will edit it.
You want to write well? Then write like this–
No, like this–
Here's another way–
Another... Fifty more!
Yet how can you read them all?
You can never read them all.
Canoe through the deltas of poetry
(for that's where our streams, or dreams, have arrived)
whose passages to the ocean–to the canon?--
are infinite, unnavigable.

****

But then there's the other side of it:
How much of the poetry even of the good poets, i.e., the recognized
and acclaimed or somewhat acclaimed poets, or the cult or coterie poets;
how much of the poetry of the poets in any and all of the various
and quite numerous divisions, tendencies, factions, schools, etc.,
of American poetry of the past fifty years–
both neglected and non-neglected--
How much of it is actually and in truth any good?!
Some days I'm not convinced that much of it is.

I'd like the "neglect" we've been speaking of
to extend far wider. A lot of hitherto unneglected,
indeed, widely admired poets
richly deserve new and specific neglects of their own.
Through rivers and mountains and other geographies, painted deserts,
alphabets, cities, migrations, harvestings, deletions, elegies, algorithms,
ingenious stanzas, other random intentions, spiritual wanderings,
nominations of demons, numbers, assemblies, samples, studies, answers,
botched inquiricals and either earnest or deft deflected, the tone of wit,
leaf-light wait for the other shoe, the other nail–
But how much, really? How much creates bliss in language?
Which of them blows the top of your head off?
Which of them looks through you?
How many are better than the movies?
Including mine; I'm not exceptional.
How many move smoothly and swiftly from excitement to dream and then
come flooding reason with purity and soundness and joy? (...not my words).
How many poems really need to be written, need (in retrospect)
to have been written–
now that they're here, now that you can read them?
How many poems, actually, in all truth,
are not frankly pretty boring?
Life is usually not boring, but poetry usually is.
Even the best poets have plenty of uninspired sits.
And often, the more renowned and successful they are,
the less critical they are of each successive poem.
Poetry is practice; yes, we know.
Poetry is craft; yes, we know.
Poetry is art; of course, certainly.
And each of these terms is a door into vast ballrooms of free and agonizing thought and effort.
Do all of it, that's all you can do; but don't think it's enough.
Most poems should be thrown away.
It seems nowadays that every poet thinks of him or herself
as their own curator.
They think, ah, where shall I donate my papers, my hard drives?!
They think, this neglect is temporary, you can take that to the bank.

They think, who is doing what I'm doing? Really! If you'd only just
read the stuff, for fuck's sake, just read it.
They think, fine, ok, I'll throw away all of it,
almost all of it,
        but just read this!

         I could have turned a hundred times.
    I remember sitting at the window of a bar on Broadway and about 109th,
        I forget the name, it's no longer there,
        I was reading, drinking a beer, it was summer,
    the windows were open, and a girl walked by on the sidewalk,
       very pretty girl, dark hair, wavy not quite curly, small, smiling.
And she looked in at me and asked, did she know me,
    and I looked back at her
          and said, no, I didn't think so.
               And she shrugged
               and smiled and walked on.
Why didn't I lie, and say, yes, I think so,
         I'm trying to remember,
           did we take a class together
at Columbia,
    or did we squeeze
       by each other at the laundromat on 107th,
     or were you at the Ashbery reading in March at Barnard?
  You look familiar, where could it be?
  Come on in have a drink and let's talk.
          In fact, both were true.
      I knew I had never met her;
       and yet she did look familiar—because in New York
    there were thousands of pretty girls who looked similar
    who had that look.
        And I'm sure that I looked familiar too.
      People were frequently telling me back
    then that I looked just like someone they knew.
         I was frequently mistaken for another.

But maybe there were several of me
         and the self I settled on was the least daring.
  Now, no one tells me I look like someone else;
      now I just look like myself, bald, with lines,
    not the sort of man to elicit erotic mistakes!
         So maybe

                  she and I had met, but in other bodies. It feels that way now.
And my failure to lie, to play,
                                  was a crucial moment in my deadening.
I can never return to her. Of course.
                                  To what can I return?

OBU Interlude #5

Why can't we be nihilists?

Why can we only be nihilists?

Why can we not be poets?

Why can we only be poets?

Because the air is not yet poisoned?

Because children are born and the burden of shared mortality is too great.

Because we see the mother cat licking her stillborn kitten for hours before she gives up, even as she nurses the two live ones.

Because our lives are lived in symbols, and mourning is both symbolic and not symbolic.

Because our sexual drives and desires wear symbolic fabric; even our nakedness is a representation.

Because one puts on and puts off; because we eat-digest-excrete; because we breathe; because at a certain point, we know we are withering; because we forestall... we exercise, we try to eat better, we become more cautious drivers, we play musical instruments or games of skill to keep our synapses lubricated and exercised.

Because it is in the absolute nature of experience to be in debt. It is essential to our being to be insufficient.

Because we are born helpless, and people must take care of us to help us grow into maturity.

Our symbolic fenestration is always cracked. It is our comic destiny to be always humiliated.

Because we are temporary.

The filing cabinet of nothing can hold everything you put in it and it will still be empty, and you can live there, and live in truth.

But there are other cabinets.

PART 4
Fables

Prior to Water

alone with it

before, where the tree
is not

There is nothing so beautiful as the tree that stands
alone

Prior to Air

their scattering
a pattern of thought

I could enunciate but then

on the branch

sliding across

fretful

the birth

OBU Interlude #4

OBU is walking in certain pastures among certain beasts.
The beasts are gentle, the beasts are predatory. The beasts have horns, the beasts have very soft but unharvestable fur. OBU is in great danger as it walks without concern through certain pastures.

The pastures are uncertain. They might actually be cities. Growing in the pasture are unseasonably tall trees. The pastures are unconscionably dense in certain places. They are dense with underground burrowing creatures. The gentle predatory beasts love to walk through forests.

OBU loves to walk through public spaces. OBU encounters fellow creatures, with whom public spaces are dense. There is density.

OBU is strangely friendly. OBU wears a smile that has a certain quality of slight uncanniness. There is a disjointedness that is not immediately apparent. OBU finds it difficult to remove its smile, to remove its strangeness, to adjust its certain quality.

And yet a layer of snow makes the city seem a pasture.

All of its eyes contain birds, gray birds. All the gray birds reject the promises that are offered to them. All of the promises lay in the snow. One of them seeks a small brown bird whose home is in the eave of a blue house.

This is one of OBU's residences. But this is an accident.

OBU promises that it will walk across the pasture; it will try to walk across the pasture. OBU promises that it will try to anticipate the underground burrows, the unexpected trees, the sudden flow of the city, the hankering for cold and for blankets when everyone lives on his or her own. There can never be enough blankets or enough unexplained tire marks that end at the edge of a sinkhole that was prematurely repaired.

There is a kingdom of voles, a very harmonious kingdom. The king is Enlightened. He has very little contact with the outside world. Pigeons are his eyes and bats are his ears.

Is Your Mirror Up to the Task?

...so you must misunderstand
in a particular way

a gymnastic disaster
a bright proverb

Language sets the terms
for its misunderstanding

Spores

1.
They have no relation to oxygen,
do not sense an atmosphere,
blurt out sentences
to the soil,
anaerobic rippling.
Light adhesive imprints
achieve variety through small errors.
      Ferns.

2.
Massive lightness. My thoughts
are a plume, a coherence of molecules
that will not disperse,
a waste product of industry:
my floating body, turning back
to address me without a face.
It swirls and settles as if in a container.
There is no container.

3.
The train goes part way, then I have to change.
Which train? Here is the end of this line,
the thick red one to the blue circle--
the stop is called "Denizen,"
There's more to go, but I am partly there,
carried on this flat carrier
as if I were dead,
but still speaking.
I sound this way because I'm here.

4.
The brain certainly has a mind of its own,
just as senses are senseless.
The denizen and the vehicle;
"He wouldn't know 'X'
if he tripped over it."
I am tripping over something.
I look down, and it's true.

5.
This instrument creates
a deft railing through the impede,
the language of the vehicle, welling
and condemning; sporadic transport
of ferns, as well as promises, contracts, wills.
Submergent sentences struggle to elongate,
rails to separate destinations.
Spores take root where they land
and begin to enunciate.
A gradual forest is instituted.

6.
I was on a path
that passed through a forest.
I was visible;
in front of me was my mother,
invisible, and behind me my sisters.
On both sides of the path
were dead and dying animals--
beasts of all kinds, large,
in agony, or still.
We walked between these masses,
following our mother through life.

PART 5
Time-Ruin-Ratio

With Ratio/In Movement//Subjective Correlative

With Ratio

with ratio
surprising the gratitude
holding flanks
in the tiny theater
jumps through our courage
as their sorrow
to sing
so incommensurate
in senses of clearness
a memory tangled
in the tiny theater

Subjective Correlative

And yet

      are

      has not flowered,

Roots branches flowers;

      a town, adjacent
            to a city, part of the city.

relations

With Ratio

            do you blue bowl
wooden spoon
larger than
Empty the space
to be pertinent is to be cookie batter
(It does jump, it does)
at the entrance she's smiling broadly
but several objects
no *thought*
have you forgotten your precision?
To pertain

Subjective Correlative

                    as "rejoicing"?
of the voice? Could it be felt
as "mourning"?
Why does it feel
how it is felt?
There is nothing abstract about
abstracted, can be
discrete and
nothing is ever still.
No shape you could call a "form."
Wind and light give color.
Some immaterial thread.
Nearby stands a tool shed.

With Ratio

Now do you

                                        Now do you

                         Now do you

Now do you

                                                    Now do you

                                          Now do you

Now do you

Subjective Correlative

                    I could have searched
For hours, for years, for a lifetime

On opening the book.
that first found my eyes
not found the words
almost clairvoyant,
Which seems
to add to the bewilderment
opening to a random page
memory
differently textured–
unraveled.
Why like this,
Why this, why this?

And each thing
that flowers
loss
of never loss
the running spectrum
Memory
the tree
of cognizance
The tree
is separate
is joined
Is separate
opens
This live thing,
it had been shut,

and then the street
the tree
Sudden cognizance
not recognized
the tree
Bent from form
the tree
disparity
Correlation

the tree
of the element
In a fraction
that flowers
has flowered

except

With Ratio

in hoof marks, lattices
in inventory, brushed trunks
in story, movement
wooded areas bordered by massed birds
congratulating with many arms
canister pavilions onto a stage of quick development
the animals as banisters
to be grieving, to jump
to be reviving in density
To be happy and regnant
in movement

Time in the Ruined House
–for Titus Kaphar and "The Vesper Project"

1.
The fire is a blue fire
like the fire in a gas range.
It seems out of control
flies from windows
consumes the house from inside.
But it also seems
if he could locate the knob
somewhere among the trees
he could turn it up or down
make it simmer.
Later, he sees the blue flame
other places, other houses.
Later, he sees the blue flame
in every atrocity's eyes,
in everything human.

2.
Time is short that's why we jump,
because the fall is so long.
There's no attention to form
in the climate suit with
external muscles.
Step from the shelf
where there is no falling.
Step into time
as a cogent bubble.
Step in again– to be reversible,
to be compounded.
In the fall, in the hovering,
in the falling, in the listening:
the sound of death in your amplified breathing.

3.
Inexplicable
was the clear evidence of an earthquake;
the house had broken in half

4.
from a fault extending miles into the earth.
Inexplicable
was how a woman's face
fell out of its portrait
to reveal another face
embedded in the wall.

5.
The picture of myself with children
safe in my arms
as the fire
extinguishes all thoughts.
When the first bomb exploded
the revulsion seemed, later,
a secret self-adoration--
the dead children's innocence
worn like a flag.

6.
What is time? Explain that–the geometry of it.
You set this up, set it in motion.
You detached the faces,
put the fetus in the belly,
opened the ground, crushed the ceiling,
made the flame of I don't know
what color take everything
into a black amnesia.
You answered the man's letter,
having ensured that only you
could have received it.

7.
In my memory of my sister's funeral
the bride woke up
too late, her husband
decomposing on a ship
in the isthmus, there was no water
the grassland was spreading
where ocean had been--
incredibly fertile, fish
still flopping.

8.
My sister was walking,
her clothes torn.
I knew not to go near her–
She glowed like algae.
I called to her, "Susan!"
Half of her face turned to me.

9.
My father ends the conversation:
"I can see this is going nowhere."

10.
Was the house insured?
What is the artist's liability?
I confronted him and said
why did you bring this poor man
into being? What did he do to you?
Are you prepared to pay
for the damaged property?
In the ruins, under a charred beam,
they found the safe.
No one knew the combination
and it sat like a closed conscience.
After the attack after the fire after the

earthquake after the revolt and suppression
after the enslavement
after the false salvation after the false
evidence after the sacred harmonic memory theater,
the documents poured out–
all of them forged of course.
As they touched the air,
the perfect reenactments of the past
crumbled into true
living forms of death.

8.
I confronted him again–
not that I saw him often.
He created brilliant works, changed lives.
And through his work he also climbed
a stairway of eminence.
I lived another life
muddled in proximities,
I could never see the end
of the present moment.
We met sometimes at job interviews.
He would ask me,
"How has your life been?
What has brought you here?"
He would say, "Do you see
that small hill, it's not so far,
from the top you'll see more."
And I looked and saw the clouds
igniting.

12.
That was the future, oscillating there,

13.
Time is proof, that's all--
proof of liability and the demand for payment;
that personal horrors correspond
to universal models.
.

PART 6

Par-oidia:
One Song Beside Another

The Art of the Future

                What makes it
                     interesting
                    are
            the changes. What makes it
                    are the changes
                       what makes
                            it interesting are
                    what makes the
                         changes what makes
                      the changes what makes the changes
                              what
                              it makes makes
                the what
                                 makes it
                    what makes
                       it
                              interesting
                    the changes
                                       changes

            the things that
              no one can do
               that people
     do
            all of them
                       thin and beautiful
            that people
                    do
                      repeating

                 and fail
                              but actually

                sexless

                            ultimately

                                          things

repeating

      speaking walking eating
             things
                    that no one can
                            do

   and so for that
               reason you want to
                            fuck them
       without sympathy

                It's just a matter
                      of such precision,
                  their beauty–

                                              in a beautiful

                                                    \

                          solemn

like children.

Mastery of technique
is the foundation of mastery.
The foundation of mastery
is funded
by foundations
of the fungible.
Thus, the avant-garde
of mastery
is established
as the technical art of the future,
universally legible,
for nothing needs to be read.
There is no gesture
that cannot be achieved.
There is no effect
that is not a gesture.
There is no voice
that lacks a voice.
There is no idea
that fails in its notation.

For the elegant cheekbones and the

                slender rounded ass beneath
                the not quite loose jumpsuit
                and the actually seductive eyes
                and red mouth are those of the
                beautiful brain damaged child
                who's lost from her parents,
                poor child in the cruel world
                no wonder she's forced
                to prostitute herself–
For who doesn't want
                to fuck a beautiful automaton
                and share in her happiness?

And so to preserve

rationality
the meaning must be

ripped
out of the content so the

gesture
can be pure and

happy
and all the

torture
will be for no

reason
and so can be seen for its

beauty.

                    The world is fucked!
                    Thank God for money!

White haired man, great genius,
plays his violin.

    Every form of consciousness
            like an immense conscience
                      seeking its emptiness

        White faces
        all his machine
        children
        no matter how
        much he loves them
        the poor things
        hateful like
        erotic lizards

And even Einstein is a lost defective child
    in the universe
    and he repeats his
    repeating
    gestures
    appropriately sad
    and brilliant
    and so empty
        that soon
    one desires him too!
    To put one's penis in his mouth
    and feel his funny mustache,
    share his visions of prisoners
    concentration camps
    big locomotives
    and anything with power

                                        or that
                        has power
                                    exerted on it:
                Like to control a bunch of people
                    and make them sing la la la
                        or make them count to three over and over
                    or make them get out of bed.

Is the microphone on?
Do you want to know what I was thinking?
The complete transformation of theater?!
That was inadvertent–of course we achieved it.
We achieved the full evacuation of consciousness
into form,
            and I, in all truth,
was only thinking
        in formal terms–
                I thought
                        to put *this*
                    next to *that*
                and let them play out
                and then two more, three more
                a full stage, always in motion;
then to swerve in parallel tangential,
                para-oidic metric
possibly aleatory, quite conceivably–
quite conceivably governed
under an unspoken rule of
the pressure of the excluded sign...
Do you see that?

But I thought then, OK, what's
        the word I'm
                looking for?
To allow for a wave? An influx?
            That would overwhelm

    a viewer's consciousness
    of the relation between
    these parts... which, really,
    is no relation, is only, or primarily
    simultaneity.

But please,
   Don't mistake
     my intentions
Don't mistake
   my invention

for
            Intention

Oh, that story
(for John Ashbery in a Bucket of Phonemes)

He never stopped keeping at it, got to give him credit for that
even after he had nothing to say, just a style in which to say it,
of coy incongruity, making believe he was some yokel of the avant garde,
some oddly costumed girl fallen onto the pizza, which could be a phrase of his,
oh ho, we all know "pizza" how did that get into the poem?
I never met him, where would I meet him, that kind man.
I saw him read, it was monotonous, he said it was important
that no one know his interpretation, which would be given away
if he put stress on particular words rather than on others, so
he placed no stress, the recitation was most relaxing, I could feel
my neck unfolding as if in a poetic session of Alexander Technique,
I felt my joints increasing their distances from each other, my pelvis
separating from my spine, and when I envisioned the poem,
which was rather long, I saw only an unscrolling whiteness,
and the poem continued as if it weren't there, so how could I
interpret it? I could only with some diffidence extend myself
toward the whiteness, which I intend, I think, with no racial
signifying, but in the sense both of blankness, primarily, and also
that "whiteness of the whale" oversignifying, the nothing that
could be all. But in this case, I don't know in that my extended self
positioned in an openness of atmosphere, detached from body,
actually grew a body around it, right there in the air and—fucking Christ!--
there was the poet still reading unvariously his promulgation
of consonances cheerfully redacting themselves.
It was I who was nowhere; everything else was finding its place
as if a meeting had just been called to order.
Everyone in the room looked sage and satisfied.
And I, it seemed from a great distance, was yelling...
[Bad lines follow and are extracted.]
"Daddy!" I heard someone call, but time circled past another promenade
and the puppies gathered wagging and chortling around the food bowl.
Magically good lines follow, but I can't remember them.

I never met him, where would I meet him.
And I never met him either, and I never met her and I
never met him or him. I did meet him once and he thought
first I could be of some use to him and then that I wasn't
very smart. And him I had as a teacher but I didn't make
much impression. And I met her and it was very nice,
I liked her as much as I liked her poems. And him I met
and didn't like him but he was old and his talent was declining.
And her I met and we're actually friends, kind of.
And him I met but he doesn't count, for several reasons.
And I met him and I don't care what anyone says, he was
a mediocre poet and a terrible teacher. And him, well I
feel I did know him well, certainly as a teacher and he was excellent
and that was good luck for me though he never bothered to help
my "career," such as it has been. And then of course there was him,
that worthless shit who really did a lot of damage
which I'm actually quite proud of having suffered.

And I was never part of the New York poets scene, I was too shy
and I didn't even know where St. Marks Church was; and I
wasn't part of the literary scene at Columbia, those shits thought my
poems were onanistic; and I never was in with the LANGUAGE gang
because I didn't know they existed till they became available for academic study;
and obviously I never hooked up with any West Coast developments
because I never visited the West Coast; and I didn't know about
contemporary Latin American poetry or contemporary French
or German poetry; and I sent poems to magazines and they
were always rejected and I sent them again and rotated them
and rearranged them and actually, and this is the truth,
they were always rejected; and I went to readings but never
talked to anyone, just like I went to concerts but I wasn't a musician
or maybe I was a musician but who would know?

But how did Ashbery live so long and apparently contentedly?
His artist friends mostly did not. There was never a moment,
I guess, when he was not looked on as a genius, not as a lunatic

and despoiler. He was both gracious and self-contained.
He had friends who admired him but were talented enough
also to push him further. He had an aesthetic place and knew
what it was. The social turmoil of his time did not, apparently,
affect him much. He knew what his world was; it was language;
it was the vectors of language through a variegated consciousness,
entering as certain given shapes, passing through, and exiting
excitedly, almost violently, inflected, in different shapes with
different velocities and directions. Almost violently, but never
actually violently. Should they have been violent? Should there
have been anger, for instance? In all of his verbal motion
and its refusal to stand still or accept a meaning one might
hang on it, the delicious imbalance and intentional imprecision
the way a painter blurs an image and creates, precisely, the smudge
that gives the precise form that's needed, and how can you talk
of imprecision.

And that was the violence, I guess–
The labor of construction could be reversed, could be
easily reversed. It was all so tentative, all in the spirit
of an essay, a putting together, could be seen as a set of drafts.
That it seemed final and formed on the page was an accident
of his ear, he just had the gift of making things sound right
and that disguised the spirit of dissolution that always inhabited
and brought to life his sentences. (In Rachel's "Drafts," the
sense of being blown apart is always evident, it's part of the form).

And so war, and racial violence and liberation, sexual violence
and liberation, the revolution of women, the struggle to remake
American culture, the American university... a reader would not
quite know all this was happening. One would know that
an enormous poetic voice had happened, there it was, listen!
Stevens and Crane have been climbed up and over; surrealism
and French modernisms enjoyed and reimagined; American
colloquial language and the language of pop culture, their illuminating
cliches and formulas embraced and rendered weird as they truly are.

His "assistants" writing their recollections in *Bomb*.
Or is it *Bomb 2*? My mentor recommended me and there I was
in the house, listening to the typewriter and soon he
dictated his letters and it was through me that his language
reached other actually existing people. For seven years
his warm references to wrongfully neglected filmmakers and composers
filled me with profound yet understated satisfaction
which only now, after his passing, can I reveal fully
in a kind of ceremony in which I pin these emoto-cultural
badges on myself. So many times I made him breakfast,
and I will note that many times he smiled when he read
the drafts of my poems.

It's all so small and slightly strange.
It's all so intricate and triple-faceted, or quintuple, it would take
if it were properly arrayed, and who really would know it
if they saw it, a thousand pages, or at least several a day
if one started early, observed the papers and blogs, perhaps took in
a cartoon as respite, or, better, remembered one from that empty
space constantly being filled of childhood.
One would subcontract it all,
or return, after all, to some single present moment
of innocence, a moment of sudden entry, without vectors.
In the greatness of one's vision, one thinks surely someone else
could also write this. Here... You give the half (or is it less?)-
written holograph to a nice person you meet at a coffee shop--
someone who seems resourceful yet modest--
and say, let's meet here next week. I will look different
but you'll know me, I'll wear a hat that says "Archie and Veronica,"
wait, no, that's from something I thought I'd thrown away into
a different poem; I'll wear something you'll recognize
because it will be yours.

Meanwhile, my old gruff visage with its still unmistakable
signs of a just vanished smile will persist arduously
yet full or ardor into your soul if ever you turn your eyes
up from the page. Stay strong, old suffragette,
your vote is safe with me, you are registered, enfranchised.

Well, that was a mangle.
The cat is chasing the bouncing ball.
Can you determine if that is a true statement?
It is plausible, yes, and it is no doubt happening somewhere, with some cat
or other, but is it true here and now, as the statement is being uttered?
And if so, or if not, does that change the sort of larger language event
being enunciated in this space?
Can we tell what is fact and what is opinion? And what is the status
of judgement? The cat is chasing the ball–fact–as a kind of simulated
hunting–opinion... opinion based on what? On a certain
knowledge of cat behavior and motivation? Thus, this utterance
is a judgement, an evaluation. But its specific truth probably
cannot be determined. The status of the play of cats,
to me at least, remains deeply mysterious regardless
of any presumed knowledge.
The barbarian saluditorians are sweeping into the public square
to exchange their hostage birds for the riches of the town,
but this demand will be denied and carnage will follow.
None of this is true or even plausible, it is entirely fantastical
and fantasy of a particularly dull sort in that it is impossible
to care about any of the posited agents.
Adjective noun verb preposition object-of-preposition infinitive
direct object preposition object-of-preposition preposition
object-of-preposition conjunction, etc. etc. OK.
Carnage? Well again, like the cat, carnage is happening somewhere.
Carnage is a word. Carnage comes from a root meaning "meat."
The transformation of living bodies into meat is happening somewhere.
It is nice to feel detached from such an event.
It is nice to have a sentence and a larger verbal structure that facilitates
detachment. Why is this true? Is it a fact or an opinion?

Seventh-grade public school teachers want to know.
It is nice to have a detached meta-cargo. Detachment might actually
be a figure of speech indicating feeling; it indicates that one *might*
feel, or that someone else might, that there are circumstances (somewhere)
conducive to strong feeling, and that outside the verbal structure
one oneself might be so conduced and that it is our good fortune
that we are not that one, that we are even in a state of almost
Wordsworthian *pre-recollection*, that we are in a special moment
just before some strong feeling might be recollected and so
our tranquility will be disturbed by something not of that nature.
We will not be tranquil, rest assured, for the surface of a pond
on which beautiful insects scurry and dragonflies swoop down
to gobble them is surely not tranquil. Our mental state will be
of that order: active, predatory but on a tiny, inhuman scale,
inordinately complex, of deep intensity.
You look up from the page and a human presence is near you, its
eyes and face, mouth in the preview of a smile, its whole visage
one of warmth. It surprises you, all of it, you think, Holy Christ,
that thing is alive! You think, how am I supposed to act? You put
your hand up in greeting. The person responds by walking to you
and embracing you. And this is a new kind of intricacy.
Put it down already, you think; down, far down, or throw it
as far as you can. The whole thing of kindness, the whole thing of desire,
and how you can put the two together, or not put them together,
and how there might somewhere be a sentence in which some of this
is true. You feel your face changing as you think of this.

PART 7

Poetics/Politics

OBU Manifesto #39

OBU concurs, with Walt Whitman, "Only what proves itself to every man and woman is so, Only what nobody denies is so."

And OBU remarks that if that's the case, then not very much is true these days, for not much is agreed on.

And OBU would like to insist on clarity and would like to put obscurity in its proper place. Obscurity is precious, it should be revered, for much that is precious is also obscure. But the beauty and value of obscurity is that the dark and hidden can cut through one as sharply as the brightest light... if one can get the language right.

And OBU repeats, "These are the thoughts of all people in all ages and lands. If they are not yours as much as ours, they are nothing or next to nothing... If they are not just as close as they are distant, they are nothing."

OBU does not believe that disrupting grammar and syntax is a revolutionary act.

But OBU feels stuck now in its terminal. It is waiting for its train, which is its terminology. Only the right terms will take it from the terminal. A term is a vehicle and a goal. A term indicates where its idea will terminate. Without the right terms, OBU fears, its progress will be only intermittent. The problem of political language and entreaty, OBU reflects, is really a problem of mobility. How do you get from one cognitive/affective place—one place of thought and feeling and experience and reflection–to another place, or the place of another. Our words for how language works are geographical. *Metaphor* means "to carry across," to carry meaning from one context to another, which means to create a new meaning that works somewhat differently in its two (or more) locations. And *metaphor* is the Greek synonym for the Latin *translation*, which means–identically– "to carry across." Every translation is a metaphor, every metaphor a translation. And every missive transmitted to another must, if it is to provide meaning, become something new as it is received. A *transmission* is something "sent across."

What wonderful neural capacities we have to do all this loading and shipping and unloading, and what amazing work it is to *understand* when symbols fly at us like barrages of balls and kites and knives and diving paper airplanes and large ungainly packages we have no idea what they are and tiny slivers of ungraspable substance that get into our eyes and nostrils like mist.

OBU is One Big Union

George Herbert wrote that prayer, the quintessential verbal jettison, was, in the end, "something understood."

OBU might be willing to consider these Manifestos as forms of prayer. But beyond all this, OBU posits, there is the untranslatable–the place withdrawn and extended outside the meaningful flux of our symbols, the things at the core and in the workings of our bodies, sensations, visceral emotions; and there are the large things, the systemic and global functions and manifestations for which our terminologies lack terminals and translations. We know what we can say about these things, and we know that we're not getting it right. We must resort to *catachresis*– the word for the thing or process for which we don't have a word; thus, necessarily, the wrong word, the word outside the network of words, the word that refuses to be carried across, that stays where it is, and you must come to it. The singular utterance.

OBU is learning to navigate.

Is this what poetry is, OBU wonders. The language that rejects all paraphrase and summary. Poetry can only be translated poorly. To translate it well requires that you transform it. People ask, what does a poem mean? And one can only answer, it means what it says. What you say *about* it is not what it means. It means what it says. Thus, you must read it. In the curved space of the untranslatable, the poem may have been sent to you (as its launch is both private and universal), but you still must go to it. It will not be where you think you saw it, and you cannot judge its location by its trajectory. Missing it one place, seek it another. Whatever is commonest and cheapest and nearest and easiest is OBU. OBU is the most obscure and secret, but OBU is tactful; it knows that not every inmost place should be illuminated.

OBU is what we bring to each other, whatever we are willing to bring.

Disintegrating Ode to a Senator

Can it be
that the coherent rational view
that served fairly well for such a long time
the useful forms
and ratios that bound the seasons,
continents and oceans in patterns

holding constant
across centuries, in fact, millennia,
and allowed, at least roughly, for planning–

the planting
and harvesting of crops,
building cities near rivers

and the mouths
of rivers, quarrying stone,
building ships, conducting trade

establishing
dynasties and other forms
of governance, even the beginnings

of democracy,
that most confident mode,
arrogant really, thinking that people

themselves, as they are,
possess the judgment to rule
a state together, in justice and prosperity,

across time-- (What
regularities and continuities
are required for that presumption!)--

Can it be
that these forms, modes, continuities of weather and geography,
levels of the ocean, flow of the rivers, chemistry of the air and water,
realities of soil and wind, the overall and encompassing predictability
of the world, the predictability of the world the adherence of the world
to models to models we humans can create and place on graphs express
through algorithms to every thing there is a season to every season there is
a set of characters you will chase through the grove with me we will be
pastoral past orality and will the form

                                                                                                  Drop

from under us and will some terrains and their atmospheres

find their

expression in fire in fire and other terrains and their

find their truth in deluge and inundation
                                                    forking the spirit of ellipse
        to in quest
            to   then to   to

and some will
            under the forming of bridge under the

gravity sudden drop
                and no lasting form of
      impervious

      There will be war soon, is that not also too obvious.

            There is not enough planet
and it

It has no

      It has no shape.

"and admit that the waters
> *around you have grown..."*
> –The Ancient Inundator

INUNDATE THE CAPITOL

Inundate capital.

In barges send the Obvious Poems, the Necessary Poems, the Inscrutable Poems, the poems made of lightening, the poems of water, the poems that resist all forms of breathing either by lungs or gills or whatever strange organs insects possess that bring them oxygen, the poems that will help you breathe again, the Obvious Poems the Necessary Poems the Inscrutable Poems the poems made of lightening the poems of water

INUNDATE the intersections where power assembles and disperses.

Send the poems in barges and container ships. Stuff the supply chains with poems.

TRANSMIT the Unacknowledged Legislation and the poems of anarchy the poems of chaos the poems of theory (of chaos, of anarchy... for there is no real chaos or anarchy, not in anything fabricated by human minds or hands, or perceived by them)

SEND the unending scrolling poems on the backs of joyous animal helpers–animal poets!–and SEND the poems created by Artificial Poets, some of them programed with arrogance and some with humility.

Poems will fill the streets of the great cities and centers of power and poets will wade through them, continually writing more.

Whitman will write to God to send picnic baskets, and Blake will write for shipments of ale, and Dickinson will contribute her endless notebooks in case anyone runs short of paper.

The rising of sea level will be exceeded by the rising of poetry level, and poems will absorb the sea and the coastal cities will be saved...

IF only we get there first.

The Unacknowledged Legislators achieved 226 signatures in their petition against Plutocracy.

A sad outcome, acknowledged by all the Unacknowledged. The petition went no further. Plutocracy endured without even noticing the challenge that would have brought it down--

Now the Poets retreat to the soil and advance both downward and upward.

Now they continue to goad the Poets of Quiescence.

The Poets of Quiescence are a tremendous power. All the potential power of the Unacknowledged Legislators resides in the anxious paralysis of the Poets of Quiescence.

What will it take to goad them? Really--What will it take?!?

Are you one of them?

Where is your small mirror in the red case that says, "What am I doing today to build a Movement?"

What am I doing today to transmit the small Incantation of Sudden Adherence that will make the waves liquid and solid that will fly through the ears and all the apertures of elected rulers

and present them with the alternative that has no alternative, the alternative of

This Is What We Have To Do

and *We Have To Do it Now.*

ACKNOWLEDGMENT.

Thank you, Poets of Acknowledgment, Poets of Inundation.

Addressing the Law

From now on I was thinking and the time has come
the time is now if time were something
to be spoken of in any polite or sociable way

and what I would do would be
to focus on *form*, the form of poetry.
I would do this because already

I had tried to imagine some, some what?
Some "interface"? What a lousy word–
some place of real actual legitimate genuine authentic
yes, connection, yes, I think so,

some connection that would involve my
language and my–ok, my self, ok–and...
What shall we call it? The "social
and political world"; I tried

pretty hard, though with uncertain and
somewhat incorrigible results
to write poems in something of the form
of missiles that would fly, as in a naval

battle (awkward stanza break there–
or was it brilliant? I have no idea...)
Flying into the side of the battle ship
of oligarchy and fascism
and conceptually damaging it,

blowing a fucking whole in its side.
Right. And all its prisoners would escape
like in *Fidelio* or *Cool Hand Luke*
and the damn thing would go down
it would just go down

conceptually, at any rate, conceptually
it would go down and the poems would
inspire others to take more practical turns
and bring it down for real;
transform this world; elucidate

and bring to light, shine the light on
the forms of mind the images of justice and
types of love that would open the door
to the solidarities we need, that we need

yes, that we need, do you understand–
that we need because we do not have;
the solidarities that we need to bring about
the society that we want. Simple as that.

The poem would announce, simply, clearly,
in all its obviousness and banality,
the unacknowledged legislation,

the *law*, the true obligation that we all
know but won't acknowledge and won't
act on, won't enforce as law.

And I thought, I've done that, I've done that,
I've done that as much as I could.

I want to experiment with form now.
I want to play with stanzas.

The world can go to hell.

OBU Manifesto #1,988

THE TROUBLE WITH OBU

is how are you supposed to read it? The name "manifesto," in spite of its lineage in literature,

is thought still to imply some political and semantic transparency.

The manifesto will tell you what it thinks. It will manifest.

It will put it down and lay it out.

The principles of OBU

The tactics of OBU

The *longue duree* of OBU.

That's how it's done.

Breton's "Surrealist Manifesto" is far from surrealist. It's actually just an essay:

"We are still living under the reign of logic: this, of course, is what I have been driving at. But in this day and age logical methods are applicable only to solving problems of secondary interest. The absolute rationalism that is still in vogue allows us to consider only facts relating directly to our experience. Logical ends, on the contrary, escape us." And much more along those lines. It's pretty clear, from start to finish, what the text is driving at.

There are more difficult instances. Take, for example, Ocalan's *Manifesto for a Democratic Civilization (vols. 1 & 2)* or Fred Moten's *Undercommons*. These are not easy to read. But their difficulty lies in their apparent need for a hyper-rigorous precision. The complexities they aim toward must be expressed with absolute exactitude. Thus, they resort to technical languages of their own invention. These are wonderful works, OBU avers; OBU is not knocking them. They are fun to read. If you like gnarly social theory and speculative history–and OBU loves 'em–they are the cat's meow. The point here is simply that their difficulty is not because their meanings or purposes are not clear.

They aim for the transparency of social science. The difficulty, especially in Moten and Harney, is that they aspire to a complex, sometimes contradictory, precision. They believe sincerely that a succinct and correct account of the nature of oppression can be articulated, and that they are doing so. If the theory can be expressed with the requisite precision, the movement itself will leap into existence (as it already exists as potential). With its defining words as weapons, it will grasp its power.

OBU is written in ordinary language. It is not precise. It is obvious. It is banal. It is not difficult to understand sentence by sentence. It has no technical language. And yet, somehow, it is harder to *read*. With Ocalan and Moten and other manifestos, you know where you stand. They are there, in a certain place, declaiming; and you are here, where you are, reading. That separation must be maintained. They are always and entirely serious. They are spelling out a theory, a correct theory. It is your job to decode the writing and get its meaning. The reader moves, or is expected to move, from his/her subjective place (the place of the act of reading) to the manifesto's objective place (the place of meaning). The manifesto is scientific. Its language is, really, an unfortunate necessity. It is a means, a medium. The goal is to see through it.

But OBU is its language. It has nothing else. There is nothing beyond it. Its meaning is its language. Its theory is its language. The experience of reading is the experience that OBU wishes its readers to have. Therefore, it must be *read*. What is then to be *understood*? What is to be understood is what happens during the experience of reading. The reader, if or as he or she is reading, is at all times inside. There is no objective other place to which the language will transport and deposit him or her. There is only here.

OBU obliterates every Archimedean point of leverage. Where are we? We're here. We're not there.

OBU fabricates and throws up its widest net and forces there to be, in the text, another place. And we are there. We are not here.

We're not. We're not. OBU is hurrying to the escape pod. It's punching in coordinates for a sector of extremely Dark Matter. The region is governed by gravities whose math has not been worked out. Why would we want to go there?

Because we can't stay here.

I Once Met Kent Johnson

I once met Kent Johnson–and this is not an exaggeration because I only met him once–that great poet–but I didn't know he was a great poet at that time, because I had never read his poetry. He was accompanied by Mr. Araki Yasusada, whose book he had edited. Mr. Yasusada refused to acknowledge my presence as I talked with Kent. Kent said, He keeps following me around. I mean, I love the book, but it's not like we have a personal relationship. He's dead, after all. And in case anyone is wondering, I did not write it.

I met Kent Johnson in New Haven Connecticut sometime in the vicinity of 2010 maybe, or maybe it was closer to 2005 or 2006. Was it before or after my children were born? I can't remember. Richard Deming might remember, or Nancy Kuhl, for it was they who brought Kent to New Haven so that he might bear witness to the witnessing of the late Araki Yasusada. So that he might bear witness to the act of witnessing to the event that he had not witnessed. Primo Levi wrote that the only true witnesses to acts of atrocity were the dead. The rest of us can only invent. In that sense, Adorno is entirely wrong about the impossibility of poetry after Auschwitz. There can *only* be poetry after Auschwitz, or there can be poetry only *after* Auschwitz, or after Hiroshima. The inhuman, the inexpressible obscene is required if poetry really is going to happen. "In the beginning" is always, really, an aftermath... If we want truth, we must die; if we want to live, we must write poems. I believe I told Kent that, or something like that. And I believe he agreed. Yasusada was silent. Yasusada then piped up and said, "You have my book, that's all I have to offer." Then he shut up again.

We sat in a seminar room in the Whitney Humanities Center at Yale. Kent was at the head of the table. Richard sat next to him. Nancy sat around the corner maybe three seats down. Do many people know how good a poet Nancy is? Richard is quite good too. I sat across from Nancy, though not quite directly across. Nancy and I always had enjoyable and instructive interchanges at these seminars. Richard and I argued a bit, but also instructively, I think. Jean-Jacques Poucell, the translator of contemporary French poetry, was there. I once went to the City Opera with Jean-Jacques and his wife, Marita. Marita knew one of the singers and so we went backstage afterward. I got to stand on the stage and look out toward the hall, toward that enormous space. Really enormous, and this was the City Opera, not even the Met. This was back when the City Opera still existed. What a glorious feeling. I wanted to start singing, to see how far my voice would reach, but I was embarrassed and didn't.

In those days, I could sing a bit; now I have this condition with my vocal cords, so my singing really is very limited. I can barely sing at all, and that pains me. I wonder if not being able to sing will affect my poetry?

Kent was talking about anonymity. Not about "death of the author" in some poststructuralist Barthes or Foucault sense. More Pessoa, of course, though I didn't know Pessoa then. It was through Kent that I discovered Pessoa. To witness what you need to witness, to give the testimony that is imperative, you must discover or create the person who will perform those tasks. When the need is great, that person cannot possibly be yourself. How could "you," as you are, write the poems that are demanded? The poet must discover the poet or the writing will be trivial, will be "personal." The personal is political, as they say, but be careful–you might be the wrong person. Kent was Kent, though; that was fairly clear. Yasusada stayed in his book. Kent read a few poems aloud, but clearly he was not Yasusada. Is the trauma there? Is the crime there? Is the death there? Where is the white flash? Is an entire life of knowledge and feeling there, somewhere?

Are you there, Kent?

I don't remember a lot of what we said, or others said.

Did I go out to dinner with you, as I assume Richard had arranged something? No, I don't believe I did. I went home.

We had had such a powerful and true conversation that we corresponded a bit afterward, but then we stopped. No more Kent Johnson.

But then. And then. Still. Ongoing. Connected by conjunctions and caesuras, crossing years.

I once met Rachel Blau DuPlessis. She once met Kent Johnson. Trump had just been elected. The idea came into my head of the "movement that does not exist" that we would need to pull ourselves out of our abyss. I began writing its manifestos. I sent a few of the early ones to Rachel, just to see what she thought. And she said, you know who might be interested in these is KENT JOHNSON, who runs a journal called "Dispatches from the Poetry Wars," and this is exactly the sort of thing he'd like. And I thought, of course! Kent Johnson, I remember him, but I didn't know about "Dispatches."

So, I wrote to Kent, and reminded him that I had once met him–though I certainly had not, at that time, read his wondrous and infinite series of poems on the poets he had met. I said, "These are OBU: One Big Union/Oligarchy Busters United." And he said, I know they are– and I once met *you*, even though you are not in my infinite series. And my series is not infinite, those were your words. And I said, true enough, but then you must also know that I have not said them yet.

And so, thanks to Kent, OBU became a thing available to be read, even though it didn't exist. And it was Kent's idea that the work be anonymous. Of course. Kent made the manifestos a bit more militant. And it's was Kent's anonymous genius as Emily Post-Avant to frame that drunken letter from the MFA student in Austin that appeared in Volume 2.

And it was Kent Johnson also who instigated the formation of the Unacknowledged Legislators: Poets for the Planet. He wrote in FaceBook, What are the poets going to do? Why aren't they burning this arid city with poems and drowning this sunken country with poems and performing fatal acts of translated or translucinated horror or desire or healing that could be actualized if only we had, a few million years ago, allowed our tails to grow along with our jowels!

And now he crosses the light. He carries it across. It crosses him. It carries him. Across. Translation is the translation of metaphor, and metaphor is the metaphor for translation.

I once met Kent Johnson. I met him once. Some indeterminate number of years ago. Years later, we became friends in words, and in the struggles of words, and in that transitive or sometimes intransitive, illuminated or obscure place between the liquid words and the solid social beaches and cliffs they crash against.

I never met a person who could hug harder in words, and who was a better friend and comrade in words.

Amor y fuerza, amigo.
Abrazos.

PART 8
Last Poems

The nut stops here. The child was there before,
scalding the future.
Let me be permeable,
let me pick up the small hitchhiker,
wading to her waist in blood and sperm,
let me carry her over.
The view to the past is clear: wombs and testicles
back to the invertebrates, infinity of ferns copulate to coal.
But it stops here.
The silent client, insolvent, the maximum
highway, the child trusting a stretched hill.
What was buoyant in fluid plummets in air.
New morning, new light, the room unchanged.
These vestibules repeat their ovulations.

Manifesto # C#minor [approximately]

Saint OBU lives on OBU Street.

OBU is streetless, it lives on dirt.

OBU cannot promulgate, it will OBUlate

and all within its witless womb will Obgestate.

OBU cannot wait. Too late

will emerge the One Big Union that does not exist

in any state and will vitiate the Oligarchy

that does nothing indeed if not exist.

OBU will sleep on a stone and preach to birds.

Its wilderness consists of words.

Its harmonies are never thirds

but sharpened demitones above the seventh.

If they could be heard they'd cut the keychain

from the Master. But their incisions are too fine.

The wound is closed before the blood flows out.

The tonic stands just registering the smallest flatness,

but who can hear it

amid the stupid laughter.

It has to be irregular.
Structure is internal,

encoded. The message
is its action, result

as division, replica
as cell sweet energy

that can gird,
frisks no matter how

empty the space
larger than--

within, so huge
from place to place

no idea or feeling
of compulsion

sudden abundance of thought
for no reason

axial thought.

OBU Manifesto #42

OBU is trudging. It is time for the trudge. Within each trudge is the brilliant flash. Or perhaps within every third or fifth trudge is the insane, precipitate, knowledge and the revelatory warmth, the feeling of connectedness with other souls. And around each flash of truth must congeal the trudge. It's the trudge that hauls for the body and the wheels, the architecture, the ability to withstand exhaustion and failure. The brilliant flash is both momentary and eternal. The trudge endures through time.

The trudge of the endless meetings; the moment finally when we have a plan and we're going to do it and keep doing it; the coordinated phone calls; the dinner with the group in another neighborhood or city; the emergency call that someone is being detained by immigration officers; the meeting with the congressperson or the state rep; the alliance of the union with the environmental group; the address to the disappointed wavering Trumpistas, and maybe two of them join you; the joining together of workers, either with or without a union, the commitment that the company will make no significant decision without the workers being part of that process; the united force of cities upon giant corporate "non-profit" entities like hospitals and universities that they contribute justly toward the cities that host them and provide them with land, labor, utilities, safe neighborhoods, clean air and water, transportation; the collective trudge that brings power to people to determine the conditions of their lives. The acrobatic leap and twist is part of the trudge. The joy of returning home having accomplished something is part of the trudge. Just the general task of life, of job and family and various enjoyments and fulfilling responsibilities, and being exhausted most of the time and being just plain sick of the whole thing and will you stop calling me, I'm tired of it, and taking the dog for a walk, getting the oil changed, suddenly having to shell out 400 or 800 bucks for repairing something or other and there's always something, and the trudge is the something that there always is. And how the hell are you supposed to do it, I mean on a continual basis, which is the standard basis; you don't generally have a choice of reducing it to something less than continual.

And the trudge is both the vision and the journey toward the vision. The journey and the vision and the work are always intertwined. And the trudge is the twine.

"The profound change has come upon them. Rooted, they grip down and begin to awaken."
OBU is and will not stop.

OBU is not about everyone thinking the same thing. Sharing a few important commitments will be enough. It's ok if you don't like *La La Land*; and it's ok if you do like *La La Land*. If you don't like *Fences*, there might be a problem

The trajectories indicated here do not stop at the end of this sentence or of this page. The energies here, both in the writing and in the reading, are propelled beyond themselves. They fly out, do reconnaissance in the future and return with vital intel.

And we'll ask ourselves when the OBU Inter-temporal Knowledge Drone returns, is that where we want to go?

One Big Union United to Bust Oligarchy and Create Democracy

What we need to know, OBU suggests, is known... all but one thing.

What I think is nothing
A fire forced me out of the house
I jerk awake like a smooth machine
and beside me a creature of wood

NOTES

1. *What is My Project?*

"What is my project?"   (*Prior*)

This question was actually asked of me, maybe twenty years ago, by Rachel Blau DuPlessis–a poet of astonishingly great projects. It's a fair question. Does a poet need some years-long, volumes-long meta-endeavor? Is just writing poems not itself a project? Take Williams as example: are *Spring and All* or *Kora in Hell* <u>not</u> projects–just books--but *Patterson* <u>is</u> a project? For me, I'd say that when, much later, OBU came into my head, that was a "project" in Rachel's sense, though I only produced two books of OBU. But did I never have a "project" before then, or since? Now I have my Naive Poetics project, and this book is part of that. This poem then addresses the question of virtuosity–not just the "project," but simply how *good* do you have to be, how skilled, how brilliant–and everyone is brilliant, it seems, present company excepted--... in order to make your "debut" as they like to say nowadays, as if publishing a first book is like going to your first ball, and you must look your most fetching in your loveliest poetic gown. I published my first book of poems in my fifties. I had already lost my hair. No one on my dance card.

"Word photons..."   (*Prior*)

Which then is the poem? The shaping of the photons to the object, or the writing set down underneath it–which is to say, the translation? The "curses and proscriptions," as in a museum exhibit, are not active or effective. Does the truth of a poem stop when it's actually inscribed? I don't believe that, and yet, yes, what it means later, when read, can be "never again/ exactly that, never again/ necessary, in that present way." Like Winnicott's "good enough parent," we make do with the "good enough poem."

"Everyone has felt it..."   (*The Obvious Poems and the Worthless Poems*)

But here's the reverse–the lyric not as transcription, but as direct breath, aolian chimes, physical emanation from a core of being. Both are true. Otherwise, there would be nothing.

"Tacit"   (*Prior*)

What is the relation between poetry and the poet's personal life and biography? I think a lot about representation and the limits of language, about alterity. I've written two scholarly books on how writers conceptualize various forms of the "unthinkable." This concern occupies much of my poetry as well. But this concern, to me, cannot be an abstraction; I have two sisters who cannot speak. Or now I have one sister alive; Susan died in 2022. The fact of their inability–have I ever, in any genre, fully grasped this, either cognitively or emotionally? However expansive, my poetry remains taciturn. I can't talk about it; I don't know what to say. I do, however, play the euphonium.

"There is always some slim girl..."   (*Prior*)

My alternative sister, my other life and other career as a poet. If I had made different choices, I would be a different person, and a different poet. Had I not transferred after freshman year from Tufts to Columbia, I would have certainly written far different poems. I make fun of that other self–he really became a not very good poet; and yet he published more than I, was more recognized, was more successful and happier. A more conventional poet. New York was too enormous. I knew no one, never fell into any group, any journal, got no praise, really, from anyone except a few friends. Koch liked my work, but never "supported" my career–I was not to be the next David Shapiro or Ron Padgett. I just kept writing and trying to get better. If I had been more "successful," even in some small circle, would I have continued to improve? Don't many poets sadly stop improving? Again, for me, the silent sister is the unacknowledged Muse. I keep writing for her.

"My Father's Questions"   (*Under the Impression*)

   This poem is an entirely true poem! This, indeed, was my dad, unashamedly sincere, a constant reader of Dickens and Shakespeare, a lawyer of taxes and estates, a founding member of the Harrisburg PA branch of the ACLU. He died in 2015. I hope it's clear that this is a poem of love, and of amusement and recalled exasperation. And I don't know the answers to his questions.

"felt–that was a plow–until"   (not previously published)

   A tiny homage to Emily Dickinson? All internal, plowed and seared, breath and touch. No public thought. None at all. A word photon poem; a lyric; its mannered inscription.

"Prior to Earth"   (*Prior*)

   How does the poem come about? Who is capable of finding it, excavating it? And then the question, who made it? What are its parts actually for? What parts are missing? What *is* the damn thing?! We look at the excavation together, the alien and me.

"Read and unread"   (*The Obvious Poems and the Worthless Poems*)

   The homonym of "read/red." Poetry is a basket of fruit, red and unred. Poetry is imprecision, throwing, bouncing–across and back, bills of lading, parcels ferried across then scattered. Where you think you are is where you were. You will eat that fruit later, when it's ripe, and repeat the last line three times, maybe jump to a ninth on the final note. And are you thinking you've heard that rhythm before? Do you feel that little pulse and don't quite know from where? I didn't either, then I did. "The white breast/of the dim sea..." Trochee. Trochee. Yes. Unread it. Yeats?! Not what was on my mind, but I've loved that line since I read it in college. "....And all disheveled wandering stars." The poem has nothing to do with Yeats. "The meaning will not be/ what you intend/ or send/ or what I receive/ and configure–"

2. *Constraints*

"Afterwit, afterearth, trembling in the buoyant–"   (*Under the Impression*)

The constraint first of form, however the form is first approached or engaged. If there are words, phrases; if there is sound or imagined (internalized) sound; if there is duration in time, finite duration, and if within the duration there are organized sequences that repeat and don't repeat–rhythms, sequences, breaks, caesuras, silences; if there are larger units of repetition and difference; if there are nets (for tennis) or walls (for squash or racket ball) or diamonds or gridirons, ovals, slopes, hardwoods, stations, terminals, cities, continents, mountain ranges, nutshells of infinite space... If there are any or all of these, there is form. There cannot not be form. There is boundary. There is circuit. "Success in circuit lies." There are lies. The utterance itself, as such. To think the form, one must be able to think beyond the form. The horizon is the form, but we know that "horizon" is an illusion of closure indicated by the earth's curvature; its circumference, its limit as sphere in space. Illusion of closure points toward real enclosure. But even the earth can only truly be thought from some point away from it.

This poem is a sonnet–the most famous poetic form. The sonnet has such long, rich, developed histories that it seems "organic." The sonnet has roots and branches, and so it seems somehow natural. It is beautiful to enter this tradition. It has a homelike feeling, like a clearing in a forest. It feels different from arbitrary form–mathematical formulas, Oulipo, Ron Silliman, things like that. I'm not so interested in those forms. How are they better? One can do anything with anything, of course. But I can't. I love sonnets more than I love algorithms. But that's just me. Other poets love other forms. I've never written a pantoun or a ghazelle.

I love "open" forms. But what exactly makes them "open"? The "open" makes a path or makes a structure. The path is melodic; the structure would be, what? Harmonic? Notes experienced simultaneously rather than in sequence... or some approximation of this idea.

I realized after I wrote "Afterwit, afterearth" that I stole some of its sound from somewhere–another constraint. It was some voice of Ashbery, who wrote no sonnets that I'm aware of. A poem from *Rivers and Mountains*, a great book of poems that did a lot to establish for me what a poem was supposed to sound like–not necessarily what it was supposed to say, but how it was to feel when you said it. The poem, "A Blessing in Disguise," ends (its last stanza, of seven four-line stanzas, a bit unusual for Ashbery):

I prefer "you" in the plural, I want "you,"
You must come to me, all golden and pale
Like the dew and the air.
And then I start getting this feeling of exaltation.

Exactly–do you hear it? "Then, cacaphonous, we can embrace, yet not renege/ our separation, that draft of half a wing–"... etc. I wanted to write a sonnet– sonnets have been a project (?) off and on for me. I love playing in those boundaries. But why, and in what form of soliciting, did I invite Ashbery into the room?

"The thing is an obstacle"   (*The Obvious Poems and the Worthless Poems*)

That's what poetic form is: negotiating obstacles, figuring out how to get around or over or under them; understanding or imagining the relation between the path and the obstacles. The goal of the poem is adroitness. Thus, the poem must be imagined as a living body, with limbs and agility, and not as a machine. The old evolutionary question: why are there no wheels in nature? Because there are no roads. If all obstacles were cleared, if the passage of language were a paved highway (kept in good repair, with no potholes), there could be no poetry.

"What it is, what it's like, what it's not"   (*The Obvious Poems and the Worthless Poems*)

This poem is dedicated to the poet and scholar Michael Davidson, and especially in recognition of his great book, *Distressing Language: Disability and the Poetics of Error*. We mishear, misspeak, and misspell. This is the happiness of language, that both sender and receiver can be wrong and no meaning can remain integral and intact. Do "accidental leanings produce meanings"? Yes! And "do accidental seemings produce gleamings"? "Is it improvisation or is it error?" "Do suppressed sluices mimic voices?" I quote myself. This is difficult to summarize or paraphrase. "It isn't a fact, it isn't an act, it isn't intact." But there *is* meaning. I still maintain that as fact and necessity. Invention, accident, and coincidence all are kin. The Guru Saussure taught us that meaning in language is produced by difference. A cat is a cat because it isn't a hat. Then put a hat *on* a cat and a piece of literature knocks on the door. Our linguistic minds *distinguish* one sign from another based on specific marks of distinction. So many signs, so many differences, so many possibilities for recombination. And therefore, so much meaning. And yet, the legacy of Saussure that made possible post-structuralism used his insight to suggest that meaning as such was impossible–that in some significant epistemological sense, the sign as such was inevitably indecipherable. Ultimately. Whenever "ultimately" might be. Why have I stopped writing in sentences all of a sudden? I prefer writing in sentences. Thinking of the Saussurean impasse of meaning cuts my utterance into fragments. By which I hope to imbue them with greater and pithier force. But this interpretation and legacy of Saussure is mistaken. Graphic and sonic difference does not result in semantic aporias; or, sure, it might, at times, and if you want to pursue them. But it need not, and generally does not prohibit meaning. The non-transparent nature of signs as symbols, their shifting and non-reductive character is what makes it possible to imagine and articulate things and conditions different from the way they are now. Symbolic thought is the thought of the alternative, and the negation. Things are not as they are. "It isn't *Tuche*, it isn't *Ananche*, it isn't Beyoncé." That's Stevens' Blue Guitar. Also Blau DuPlessis' Pink Guitar. It's not that nothing has meaning. What a stupid idea. Everything has meaning. For real. It's true.

"It Takes All Kinds, But It Doesn't Take Much"   (*Under the Impression*)

More along these lines. Variations on a cliche–on two cliches--as vehicles of some sort of truth, while in thrall of, or in love with, sequences of silly rhymes. "The kin of the kind." Again, sonic, formal resemblance–and what significance could possibly follow from that arbitrary semblance? Kind, rind, mind, innerly designed. And the obvious pun: kind as type, kind as kindness; kinship as moral and aesthetic principle. And can any form of judgement come into play? "If there were to be / generalized kindness, how could we tell one kind from another?" Perhaps there's no need. Perhaps judgement can be a function of play! Allow for plenitude. What would it take for life to assume its true nature as dance? It would take more than we have, of course, much more, much more. This is an exceptionally needy poem. It searches for its mother

"I Filled in My Form"   (*Under the Impression*)

Oh, those young poets–and even some older poets. What forms they produce and bring to the world. Stanzas like membranes, exploding in joy, the art of plenitude and dissolution. Continue, continue! And then achieve fame, become affable and ponderous. My cynical, envious character jumps onto the page. The more intelligence, the more stupidity. "What would it mean for poetry to be a privileged form of knowledge?" How the fuck should I know? I have no idea. I don't even know what it means to ask the question. I just asked it because it sounds like the sort of thing that smart people ask. The whole thing pisses me off. I'll invent a new form. Oh, too bad, somebody else already invented it, and they have more friends than I do and are better looking. What is my constraint? My obstacle? My algorithm? Just the fact of the limits of myself, my ability, my courage, my reading, the time I'm willing to put in. The joke of my considering myself a decent poet. My cleverness.

"will be code [this]"   (*The Obvious Poems and the Worthless Poems*)

A perfect poem: formal and abstract. Coded code. Read it. It says it, it's right there. It's in couplets, but was not always in couplets. It was very different, began as something far more garrulous and winding, expansive. But there was nothing there. Now there's something. There's it. *It*. I put it there. I crushed all the fluid out of it. I forced it to be an object.

"I Fell for the Bread Nurse"   (*Under the Impression*)

This is the allegory of form and love–the story of the creation of bread and the union of nourishment and nurture. "I felt I could not rise/until she kneaded me"! Yes, "rise" has, obviously, the meaning you think it has; likewise the pun on "kneaded.". What is "the oven's orthodoxy"? The volatile and mobile dough must take its form, and retain it. What had been an excess of feeling and volubility– "When the Bread Nurse smiles,/ no architecture/ of ligaments can hold/ its cantilever"–at last is given shape, baked, and rises in joy. What is the Bread Nurse? Only the object of desire and the agent of form. For a poem to come into being, there must be desire–both erotic and infantile; desire for the lover and for the mother–and there must be the active, intentional, improvisational, fermentative, and traumatic process of giving shape. "The Bread Nurse formed me/ then she baked me." She is that enormous world of being in which the self is lost and the created, shaped thing of art is born. This poem owes some of its mood to Maurice Sendak, especially his book *In The Night Kitchen*, which contains no Bread Nurse herself, but shows exemplary joy in the fantasy of creation within anarchic structure.

3. Anthologies of Neglect

"If I Only Knew"   (not previously published)

These are the sad, frustrated poems. Part of my life as a poet–true of most poets–is to think this whole process and vocation is a bunch of crap. I'm mediocre. Or maybe I'm better than mediocre, but no one else seems to think so. And I think back, remember when I was young, in college and my twenties, and I thought I was pretty good, maybe, and that I knew a lot. Hell, I went to Columbia; I studied with Kenneth Koch. I wanted to know more and more. I wasn't complacent. But I thought I had something going and it was only a matter of time, and not so much time, I hoped, that people in Poetry World were going to notice. And I was wrong, wrong about everything. I didn't know very much, really; and the recognition that I longed for and expected, and that meant everything to me never really happened. This poem spells that out, perhaps a bit poignantly. But then it's got that snap at the end. Because I was so stupid; because I really didn't know that I didn't know... I had the bizarre, misplaced confidence that I could do anything! And so, since I was in fact incapable of facing reality, I was free to continue to write and to explore and to learn... gradually, over years, always in a struggle to write better, and trying to convince this person or editor or other that, yes, I can write! The poem says it better: "I would have seen that my grand belief horizon/ was a pile of sticks, a barricade/ of assumptions assembled in fear and impatience." But that's what let me keep writing. The "pile of sticks" comes from Lars van Trier's movie *Melancholia*; the little structure built at the end of the film as the world is about to end–its purpose is to convince the little boy not to be afraid because he and his mother and aunt will be in a "magic cave" that will protect them. I didn't think of this as I was writing. But afterward, I realized where the image had come from.

"What's Dead on the Page"   (*The Obvious Poems and the Worthless Poems*)

What's there to say? Invention to no end; that is, no purpose... or no ending. Ranting in puns and non-sequitors, interruptions and obliviated punctuation. "Cutting the edge poor edge./ Mirrors are mist obscurity wears paint." The funeral march of language, one thing after another, engraving.

"Time is Passing and I'm not in the Groove"   (*Under the Impression*)

The problem again, in another version or reversal. There it is, there is something, and it's alive, it's changing. But in the micro-moment between perception or sensation–the inner, neural experience of the thing–and the lurch to record, interpret, (mis)understand, represent... the entire thing is lost and is something else. It's trying to improvise in a jazz song that's too hard for you– the chord changes come too fast, the rhythms are too tricky, you can't hear where a damn measure begins because every hit seems to be on an off-beat. You don't know where you are. And so you're left desperately listening for the Symbol that will orient you.

"Someone Else Might Like This"   (*Under the Impression*)

How many ways are there to ruin the poem? Bad images or not enough images... You need more *images* in the poem. People say that a lot, but it's wrong. Uninventive language, certainly. But the problem is not seeing, but hearing. The bad poem, mostly, is rhythmically bad. The poet has no ear. The poet doesn't grasp the difference (can't hear the difference) between a stressed and an unstressed word or syllable. Where Does the Poem Put its Emphasis? If you can't establish what needs to be emphatic, then the poem can't exist as a temporal semantic object. It will not flow. It will not cross the street or swim across the river or climb a mountain or descend into a valley or take the elevator or stand on a balcony or run as fast as it can or fall on its face. It can do none of those things or infinitely more; and all because it can't hear how some words, syllables, phrases must be given emphasis over others... which means to create rhythm. The bad poem "lacks a presence in the muscles, that's the real jump, that's the place/ the poem would begin, if a poem could fit there." The poem is kinesthetic correlative, already a synecdoche of itself, already in its posture and gesture, its ambulation, a moral fable. The poem is a story of life in motion. "It's necessary that you see it, but only because of where it fits/ with the entire system, that you can never see..."

"Anthologies of Neglect"   (not previously published)

This poem emerged in response to something that Kent Johnson posted on FaceBook, back when he was alive, in the last year or two of his life when he made FaceBook posts into a literary genre and instigator of real conversations about poetry and politics, and the politics of poetry–a task that no one has been able to take over from him. I don't recall exactly what his post was, but it must have had something to do (as many of his comments did) with poetic hierarchies and who determines them, and of course the ways in which all of us poets suffer such anxieties and frustrations about our places in those pecking orders. I think of Kent's wonderful and ridiculous poem about never having a poem of his selected for the annual "Best American Poetry" anthology! ("Could Someone Tell Me Why" in *Because of Poetry I Have a Really Big House*). And I've been thinking, it's wonderful and inspiring to have such varied poetic ecosystems and all these flourishing local scenes where people read and there are open mics and small magazines, cliques and friend groups, mutual admiration societies. And most of the poems produced in these scenes are–well, what are they? Inept, amateurish, revealing woefully insufficient knowledge of the history of poetry, especially of modern poetry. And yet, these products are also the products of unquenchable love of poetry and of the pleasure in putting words together. "The kelson is a creation of love," wrote Whitman; and all these bad poems are, I think or sometimes think, the foundations and nourishing soils for all the poems written by better, more sophisticated poets. There are never enough poems, good or bad. Or, conversely, there are too many poems under any circumstances. Too many lousy poems. Even poets who have written excellent poems are capable of writing bad ones. And once these poets achieve a certain stature, their bad poems will be published with as much credibility as their good ones. And, at that point, what's the difference? And hey! What about *my* poems??!! And in the immortal words of Nathan Lane in *The Producers*, "WHO DO I HAVE TO FUCK TO GET A BREAK IN THIS TOWN???!!!" Not that that would be a special incentive to anyone at this point in my life.

"I could have turned a hundred times"   (*Prior*)

Again, why did I go this way rather than that way? Why did I not take more chances, in life and in writing? Why was I not a better liar?

"OBU Interlude #5"   (*The OBU Manifestos*)

This is a great poem, goddammit. I am a fucking deep motherfucking poet.

OBU is a thing I invented just after Trump was elected in 2016. One Big Union/Oligarchy Busters United. OBU is the Movement That Does Not Exist, brought into nonexistence at the realization that none of the movements, parties, factions, NGOs, etc. that *do* exist were capable of hauling us out the abyssal ditch we had driven into. *The OBU Manifestos* (published on Dispatches Editions/Spuyten Duyvil Press, 2017) consisted of forty-two manifestos and five "Interludes," which read more like "poetry," though still having some "manifesto"-like qualities. This one is something of a "defense of poetry." We write poetry because... we don't have to be nihilists. We *can* be nihilists, and there is certainly a logic and justification for that choice. But you don't have to. You can be a poet for the very same reason that you can be a sentient, conscious, mortal, sexed, symbol using being. You can be a poet because that's what we are; or, that's one thing within the biological-social range of human possibility. But I don't know what it means. I don't know what we can do. What will it take to pull ourselves out of this abyss? Only everything we have, all we can bring, every tool we can carry and imagine.

4. Fables

"Prior to Water"   (*Prior*)

The poem's *anterior*. "Stop this day and night with me and you shall possess the origin of all poems," wrote Whitman, and he was joking and not joking. To discover that place, not a place of language, that is *prior*. *Prior* is the title of my first book of poems, from which this poem is taken. There are poems titled "Prior to Water," "Prior to Air," and "Prior to Earth." What would words be if they weren't words? What could consciousness be if it did not have language to give it focus and structure? "To be like the animals, but to think," said Doctor Matthew O'Connor in Djuna Barnes' *Nightwood*. Of course, animals do think; the doctor meant, think symbolically. Lacan asserted that the unconscious is structured like a language. Is this hyperbole? Freud referred to "primary process" which operated prior to the intervention of language. But how far down does it go? And once you have moved deeper than the reach of that cable, where are you? What medium fills your lungs? These poems are fables, in the zone of the fabulous, the fabulated. They stand for what isn't there.

"Prior to Air"   (*Prior*)

I have often said, when pondering the question, "what does a poem mean?", – *it means what it says*. I think this is true, though obviously flip and tautological. Prior to the elements, givens, a prioris, and Kantian categories of this world, the *signs* for the unsignified (the "phenomenal"?) would seem to be minimal. The "minimal," as a poetic-stylistic decision is the stand-in, the catachresis, for what is prior to signification (and representation and meaning and form). But I've put it in words. The "current words..." There's a wonderful moment in Conrad's *The Secret Agent*. Two anarchists are conversing and find themselves quibbling over the use of the word "crime." One of them, in frustration, exclaims, "How am I to express myself? One must use the current words." Poetry, we might say, is a discourse that opposes the "current words" insofar as they exist necessarily in current ideological contexts. And yet, they are words nonetheless, all of which remain in that flexible network of words. We may, like the L-A-N-G-U-A-G-E movement, insist on continually exposing the ideological semantic and syntactic shells that inhibit the uses of language that might be characterized as free. Break those shells, imagine a language unshelled of its ideology; both prior to and post ideology. That was done. Was it especially convincing even in a political sense? Largely not, I think. From Charles Bernstein's "I and the" (from *The Sophist*, 1987):

brother hmmm appointment
middle connected hit
uptight itself questions

whom boys area
excuse vacation normal
died sound subject

obvious store mother's
discuss became react
everyone beautiful noticed

The poem is twenty pages long. Its format of three line stanzas with three words in each line derives from the frequency in the use of words in 229 psychoanalytic sessions spoken by twenty-nine speakers—in descending order of frequency. Interesting effects? Maybe. Sometimes. It's really an AI exercise, isn't it? Poetry according to program.... to prove that it can be done, that poetry can be created according to entirely different rubrics and origins that completely bypass any reference to subjectivity–ah! except of course for the fact that these words were used by patients in psychoanalysis, in "talk therapy." These would be the important words, though removed from their contexts of use. Subjectivity as removed as if surgically from its status as subjective! Very neat trick, actually. This removal is crucial insofar as the "subject" can only be conceived as an ideologically inflected construction and thus the subject's utterances can only likewise be ideologically inflected. Poetry is recreated as non expressive, non representational, non discursive, non aesthetic: and in this way (and other related ways) no longer part of the larger symbolic apparatus of capitalist oppression. This can be done. There it is. Even the discourse of psychoanalysis can clatter into stanzas denuded of the personal, perhaps of interest to social scientists looking to determine what really is of importance to these test-subjects.

As you can tell, I was not attracted to that mode or impulse toward disjunction and estrangement... but, rather, toward other modes and impulses. I remember when I was writing the "Prior to" poems, I was reading Celan, who tried in an utterly different way to rip poetic language out of current shapes. He sought, however, to push his language toward more intense expression and certainly not to steer it away from some rigid idea of lyric "expression" that must be critiqued and overturned. Here's a short, late poem:

JANUARIED
into the thorn-covered
rock recess. (Get drunk
and call it
Paris).

My shoulder frost-sealed,

silent

rubble owls perched on it;

letters between my toes;

certainty.

That's more of what was in my ear. What does it mean? Is it a kind of fable? Who is its subject? "Subject" I use as a technical term. It means the place that generates the poem. The human person who is the poet discovers encounters invents needs and creates the need for the "subject" that then generates the poem. The poem and its "subjectivity" is defamiliar(ized), but not, and *never*, detached. To be detached would be an obscenity.

I apologize to Charles Bernstein for juxtaposing his poem to Celan's That was unfair. I like Charles as a person and admire him as a remarkable thinker, writer, and wit. The direction of poetics he helped launch was a brilliant provocation. It's a foil, for me; an obstacle. It helps give a form to my thinking.

"OBU Interlude #4"   (*The OBU Manifestos*)

The dream of threat and reconciliation, of predation relieved of its necessity. A fable of the impossible imagined as imaginary. If the impossible is only imaginary, perhaps the possible can be real. The poem is committed to the possible and the real, but must use the language of the impossible and imaginary. This is the meaning of a fable. The predators are gentle, uncertain, uncanny, and engaged in gentle, uncertain, and uncanny social relations. All is hovering and ascendent. Harmonious. Impossible. Part of OBU's utopian insistence. All that is now proved was once only imagined.

"Is Your Mirror Up to the Task?"   (not previously published)

The task of mimesis?!

"Spores"   (*Prior*)

Another poem of origin and dispersal. But what is that moment between the two, or are they instantaneous? I mean simultaneous; or within an instant of each other, thus indistinguishable. "A coherence of molecules." My mother died nine years ago. One of my two sisters died last year, no, it was two years past. I think of those lives and deaths when I read the poem now. "...following our mother through life." Of course; another of my cherished tautological banalities. We don't know where we're going; seeds are blown everywhere; or spores, which are single-celled and nonflowering, producing ferns and mushrooms. "Spores take root where they land/ and begin to enunciate." I guess I'm a spore of sorts. Poets as spores; humbler than seeds. Sometimes we can be seeds, and our poems will be flowers and fruits, and will nourish themselves in air and sunlight. But mostly we're spores–anaerobic, living on debris, without photosynthesis. Through all this, the story goes back to the family story. My sisters, my mother, "on a path that passed through a forest." Here and gone. And I have children now, as I did not when I wrote this poem.

5. Ratio and Time

"With Ratio/In Movement//Subjective Correlative"
(*The Obvious Poems and the Worthless Poems*)

This poem is two sets of intersecting poems, seven poems in all. It is formal, abstract; except it's not. It takes no form; its details, phrases, referents are concrete. No abstraction is truly abstract. And, in language, nothing "concrete," could possibly be concrete. People refer to the "materiality" of language, and yes, it is audible and, as writing, it is visible; and these materials of sound and inscription can be played with and are material to construct the poetic artefact. But the sense of the poem–that is its signification, its meaning or what it is taken to mean–is not "concrete" or "material." "Sense," of course, in this sense (context) is a pun. Thus, immediately, there is relation between material and immaterial–and there is movement between the two. There is action, mental action; there is ratio.

This set of poems is in the book *The Obvious Poems and the Worthless Poems*. It is in the section of "worthless poems." The "Obvious Poems" are about politics in our current era in which our political vessel, like that enormous barge in the Baltimore harbor, lost its power of navigation and drifted ever so slowly and yet with such unimaginable mass into the bridge of an Interstate highway that then collapsed entirely within seconds. What can be said about our current political impasses, our crises that are both shocking and utterly predictable... what can be said that is not completely obvious? Thus, the Obvious Poems. And once the frustration at continually stating the obvious at last overwhelmed me, I gave up on trying to engage with our politics and turned to formal experiments and also to more "personal" poems–about my life, my family, my feelings. And what, I thought, in the current circumstances, could be more worthless?

The first poem, "WITH RATIO," presents "the tiny theater" in which this action takes place. The tiny theater contains everything: courage, sorrow, clarity, memory, the incommensurate. It is a list and a composite of relations. The nouns or concepts are connected by small verbs: holding, jumps, to sing, tangled. The poem is static and in motion; or, it is a structure that contains actions; it contains the words that designate actions, though there seems to be no source of agency. Then what is there? I just yesterday came across a famous quotation from Kafka that I somehow had never seen before: "Alle Sprache ist nur eine schlechte Übersetzung." All language is nothing but a bad translation. But the words, as the instruments they are, pick up some essential part of the rhythm and tune of what is improperly being carried across, and so catachresis arrives in its proper disguise as metaphor. So, there is something understood–if only as a set of relations.

The second poem, "SUBJECTIVE CORRELATIVE." Again "relation," but now detached, beneath, an *underthought*. The poem begins with a conjunction, "And yet." It passes through a plural static verb, "are," to a quick scene of vegetation, germination, the processes of vegetable growth–but not yet. One more wonderful thing about language is that once you have presented an idea or picture in words, even after you've negated it, it remains. The poem says, "has not flowered..." But there are the flowers. This is not the case in real life. The poem refers to a town, then a city, and a relation between the two; the one is both adjacent to and part of the other. This sounds like Oppen, I think, that great articulator of the abstract-concrete. "The emotions are engaged/ Entering the city/ As entering any city."

T.S. Eliot, of course, developed the idea of the "objective correlative." This is a strange theory, that an emotion should be able to be completely expressed through its correlation with a poetic image. The objective correlative, Eliot wrote in an essay on *Hamlet*, consists of "a set of objects, a situation, a chain of events which shall be the formula of that particular emotion; such that when the external facts, which must terminate in sensory experience, are given, the emotion is immediately evoked." Thus, "artistic 'inevitability' lies in this complete adequacy of the external to the emotion." This seems an astonishing idea–astonishingly wrong! An image or whatnot will be a "formula" for a feeling that is both intended (and felt?) by the author and *inevitably* then felt also and identically by the reader! Who really can believe this? (And who can take seriously Eliot's no doubt purposefully shocking evaluation of *Hamlet* as an artistic failure?!). And yet, works of art do evoke emotion, and it seems–has often seemed to me–that there is some inevitable quality to this experience. You read or hear or see some work of art, and bang!–the effect of it is both emotionally elevating and devastating, and also seems to have the power of a syllogism; it just cannot be denied or avoided. There it is, before you and now within you, like a fact. Once you've experienced it, you're not the same. But there's nothing objective about it. Another person may apprehend the work and feel very little. It's a matter of conjunction: the art's formal substance, its subject matter, one's own experience and biography, the context of the moment of encounter. There's a lot getting correlated. And that set of conjunctions, I'm imagining, is the "Subjective Correlative."

The third poem, "WITH RATIO." The open ending, "To pertain"... which may or may not follow from, "to be pertinent is to be cookie batter." What does it take to be pertinent? "(It does jump, it does)." Is that a slight riff on a Billie Chernicoff line... "I greet, I praise/ and receive him, I do"? No, I wrote my poem before I read hers.

The fourth poem, "SUBJECTIVE CORRELATIVE." How does a poem hold together? And why and how does it have any effect at all? To feel sadness through art gives us joy, as Aristotle said, though not exactly. I just found an article on the NPR website called "Understanding the Joy that Many Find in

Sadness," and that truly made me sad—what awful, trivial thinking about the most profound question of aesthetics. I won't even go into it. Neuroscience. Well, duh. And what isn't? I'll just say again, "Why does it feel/ how it is felt?" I don't know. "What's Hecuba to him or he to Hecuba, that he should weep for her?" I don't know that either. And what makes a shape into a form? What is the "immaterial thread"? Is it obvious, then, why the poem ends with that tool shed standing nearby? I think so. Again, a little Oppen in the middle of the poem? And the tool shed is Williams!

The fifth poem, "WITH RATIO." There is the unanswered question, and there is the uncompleted question. It doesn't know what it is asking. It doesn't know what to ask. But the question is urgent; it must be asked *now*. And it is addressed to someone specific: it is addressed to *you*.

Now do you *see*? Now do you *understand*? Now do you *acknowledge*? Now do you *enter into some formative relation with*? Now do you *look inside yourself*? Now do you *embark*? Now do you *arrive*? What? Now what do you do? "What the study could not teach—what the preaching could not accomplish is accomplish'd, is it not?" A very open question—a passage over a river. Now do you...? Collapse in weeping? Rise in joy through the oven's orthodoxy? Suspend yourself? The measure of the question is a hinge. Seven times it insists, it swings open, open.

The two halves of the poem merge—they were never separate. The ratio *is* the correlative. The feeling is the measurement.

The sixth poem, "SUBJECTIVE CORRELATIVE." Recognition; re-cognition. In Spring, the trees flower; in memory, the trees flower. In art. In selection, in mimesis, in refraction, redaction, error, exception. Sublimation: to create as sublime; also to repress. "The tree/ of cognizance"/// "Sudden cognizance/ not recognized." The concrete particulars, as we call them... but, "Why like this, Why this, why this?"

The Seventh poem, "WITH RATIO." The poem moves, it moves. It loves its verbs. It loves its nouns. It loves its prepositions. It loves its participles. It even loves its adjectives. It loves its misappropriations. It loves its harmony. The poem moves, "happy and regnant/ in movement."

"Time in the Ruined House"   (*Under the Impression*)

This poem is for the great American artist, Titus Kaphar (b. 1976) and his extraordinary installation, "The Vesper Project" (2013; Friedman Benda Gallery, New York NY). The installation is of the ruins of a house. The house has collapsed on itself, but there are spaces in it that you can walk through. There is furniture, mostly smashed. Most everything is smashed. There are picture frames with missing pictures, or with pictures that have been damaged strangely: faces missing from portraits, faces with just the mouths covered in black. The ruin has a story. It dates to Reconstruction. A light skinned Black man, Benjamin Vesper, is "passing." He is discovered; there is violent reprisal. Years later, a descendent living in Connecticut, now in a mental institution, contacts the artist. Something of the story, as far as the man can recall it, emerges. The artist constructs the house and all the ruin within it and beyond it. Some of the story is the Vesper story; some of the story is Titus' story. Titus' story emerges out of the Vesper story, and yet he, the artist, invented the Vespers. The violence of American racial history transmits itself and is continually felt and reimagined by each generation. The installation of ruin is the vehicle of transmission.

One of the first lines of the poem that I thought of became the poem's final line: that "Time is proof... that personal horrors correspond/ to universal models." The ruin of a people is built through the destruction of individual lives. And the ruin refuses to speak. It has no power of speech. Of course, it is "semiotic." It signifies. But what? Something like Benjy's wailing in *The Sound and the Fury*? ... "It was nothing. Just sound. It might have been all time and injustice and sorrow become vocal for an instant by a conjunction of the planets." But no, it's not that. The ruin is not cosmic. It is matter. It is extraordinarily detailed. Every particular of broken life has been made and placed there. It is not nostalgic. It does not express longing for a lost sister. It does not repress the memory of violence. So, no, not Faulkner, though those lines came to my mind. But the twining of personal and historical animates the art.

My poem tries to extend that twining. I imagine the Vesper descendent as real–and yet as the invention of the artist. The artist imagined him in order to destroy him, to bring about his insanity–the insanity of a history experienced as too real, as a ruin unable to be set to the side so that life might continue. What an act of cruelty! Poor unreal man. (Synecdoche).

And I imagined my own stories taking residence in the ruin; trespassing, I guess. But I also have stories that resonate with ruin, that I seldom tell: the stories of my sisters. My sister Susan in particular, though she was alive then. Her funeral was invented, and her reanimation as a sort of zombie on the isthmus. My father's curt dismissal, which was a phrase he said once, when he was quite old and we were arguing about something. Unbearable pain somehow transfers itself into a work of art–both general, historical pain and personal pain. The artist who orchestrates these movements stands in some extra-moral capacity. The ruin must be built. Those who suffer must suffer. But it's art! But it's art! Yes. Of course.

The installation is a massive instance of Subjective Correlative. My poem is a small mimesis.

https://www.kapharstudio.com/the-vesper-project/

6. "Paroidia"–One Song Beside Another

"The Art of the Future"   (*Prior*)

A parody takes the form and style of a work and uses it to create a mockery. The original text is serious, widely regarded as serious–and appears to take itself with enormous seriousness. It is a work of vision and genius that defines its moment. The parodic imitation reveals this seriousness as ridiculous posturing. The artist is a pretentious, self-satisfied fool. Here are his ridiculous techniques; here is the real work of art once its pretenses and postures are unmasked. The parody is the mocking of someone else's poetics, the disguised substitution of, presumably, one's own–disguised as the object of its mockery.

The Robert Wilson/Phillip Glass opera *Einstein on the Beach* was first produced in 1976 in Avignon, France. I first became aware of the work when it was produced at the Brooklyn Academy of Music in 1984. It received an enormous amount of attention and, mostly, extravagant praise. All the contemporaneous avant-gardes of musical composition, poetic language, dance, theatrical staging came together as late twentieth-century *gesamtkunstwerk*. It sounded intriguing. I was interested in all those arts. I was, at that time, going to a lot of experimental theater and dance and music performances in New York. I was even studying dance myself and doing some theater performance approximately 10 to the 12th power off-Broadway. And there was *Einstein on the Beach*.

I couldn't get tickets. I never saw the show. But—PBS filmed a documentary about the show's production, with a lot of extended sequences from the opera and a lot of interviews with Glass and Wilson. So, I watched the documentary, and I thought, what an inflated, pompous, self-important, pretentious, repetitive amalgam of avantish emptiness. Yes, that was my impression. Technically brilliant, without question. Every detail of it was absolutely perfect. And one could also see the money that went into it. It was an opera, and operas cost money; it's the most expensive branch of theater. But *Einstein*?! Here was the fringe now arrived at the center. How had Glass and Wilson gotten this level of funding? It was astonishing. Technique at the highest level plus funding at the highest level. I felt an overwhelming arrogance to the whole project, a feeling that grew as I heard Glass and Wilson talk. My God, what ponderous windbags of theoretical blather. And yet, it seemed that their success forestalled all criticism. Here we are, they seemed to say: We've assembled the best talent in the world, and money just flows to us. So, if you've got any problem, you can kiss our avant-behinds. This is the State of the Art. We've just defined it.

And I just thought, Wow! Right. Forget La Mama, forget Richard Foreman's Ontological-Hysterics, the Bread and Puppets can spread their garlic up in Vermont, George Crumb can play to his two-bit audiences at 116th Street. Avant-garde performance had at last achieved the status of avant-garde visual art: that is, it had fully become commodity. Fuck it. I'd rather see a Rococo-inspired pie eating contest.

And so I wrote "The Art of the Future." I tried to emulate the formal repetitions, or variations as repetitions of the music and staging and what I took to be their semantic-ethical emptiness. And I also inserted what seemed to me a very apparent subtext—or not "sub," but quite open aspect—which was *Einstein's* strange eroticism—the perfect and apparently mindless beauty of the performers. Physically perfect people performing mindless actions. There seemed something strangely, perversely sexual about it, a mechanical quality. There's probably a Lacanian way to describe it. Or it might be compatible with the old (which then was not so old) Deleuze-Guattari "desiring machine" from *Anti-Oedipus*.

But whatever it was, it seemed ostentatious and pointless. But still pretty sexy, actually. That's one of the strange things about sex; it doesn't matter how stupid it is, if it can intercept the right synapses, it's got you.

I also tried to get the flavor of some of the pompous interviews. The guys are so cool, so completely situated in their primacy. Mountains of the Insufferable.

I did a bit of revising of this poem for this edition–far more than I did for any other poem in the book. And mostly, I revised the interview parody sections. Reading them again, I didn't feel I'd gotten them right. Or maybe I did, and I'm wrong now. But even if they were more accurate in the original form, I didn't like how they sounded as part of the poem. I gave them a little more serious, ponderous a voice, and I reconceived the ending a bit.

"Don't mistake/ my invention/ for Intention."

Well, yes, I thought to parody what seemed to me an irresponsible abdication of meaning, a pretentious coyness. But I question "intention" too, as I've made clear. I see where intention can veer, and I try to make use of those shifts, and I try to make myself sensitive to the forces and environments that bring them about. To allow invention to play apart from intention has to be one of the true bases of art. But if some relation to meaning is to be preserved, and if invention ultimately (and I would insist that "ultimately" is a long time!) has some important relation to meaning, and meaning to ethics, then invention and intention are entwined. Sometimes "intention" can be mistaken for "invention."

It also occurs to me that maybe I really fundamentally misunderstood *Einstein on the Beach*. After all, I didn't actually see it. I saw the documentary and I apprehended the opera's large cultural profile. But maybe my parody is of an idea I came up with and not of the Glass/Wilson text. It's possible. So many people think so highly of this work. But then, some years later, I saw a production of one of their subsequent operas, *Akhnaten*. I guess it was at the Metropolitan Opera in 2019. Again, an immense, meticulous production. And this opera has more of a narrative than does *Einstein*. But again, it seemed to me pretty empty and pretentious.

Parody must contain some portion of malice.

"Oh, that story (for John Ashbery in a Bucket of Phonemes)"
(Under the Impression)

The poem's title, as all fans of J.A. recognize, refers to his poem, "The Picture of Little J.A. in a Prospect of Flowers," one of his most personal poems. It ends,

...Though I was wrong,
Still, as the loveliest feelings

Must soon find words, and these, yes,
Displace them, so I am not wrong
In calling this comic version of myself
The true one. For as change is horror,
Virtue is really stubbornness

And only in the light of lost words
Can we imagine our rewards.

And Ashbery's poem refers to Andrew Marvell's "The Picture of Little T.C. in a Prospect of Flowers," a poem to a young girl, of praise and, at times, admonition. Here is its first of five stanzas:

See with what simplicity
This nymph begins her golden days!
In the green grass she loves to lie,
And there with her fair aspect tames
The wilder flowers, and gives them names:
But only with the roses plays;
And them does tell
What colour best becomes them, and what smell.

And here is the start of Ashbery's poem:

Darkness falls like a wet sponge
And Dick gives Genevieve a swift punch
In the pajamas. "Aroint thee, witch."
Her tongue from previous ecstasy
Releases thoughts like little hats.

Parody must contain some portion of love.

Why is parody important to a poetics? Parody is a deep engagement with a text. It is a kind of close reading. It is a distorted imitation, a forged ventriloquism. It is a caricature that reveals true features. It must contain malice. Ashbery's "Picture" is certainly a reading of Marvell's "Picture"–with more love than malice, I think, though Marvell's "nymph" seems to have been turned into a "witch." Is Ashbery's poem even a parody at all, or more of a stepping off from an example of a poem of childhood that Marvell offered and that Ashbery accepted and transformed. My poem, however, *is* a parody of Ashbery's style and sensibility–turning "a prospect of flowers" into "a bucket of phonemes."

And I love John Ashbery's work. Ever since I first read it–I think my first book of his was *Rivers and Mountains*–his voice has always been in my head. His voice has been the most powerful and original voice in American poetry since WWII. Hasn't it? I had to work to get out from Ashbery's voice, its mix of deep seriousness (sometimes an affectation, or parody) and colloquial silliness (sometimes an affectation, or parody); intellect and levity; a continual flow of mental-linguistic charged particles–and yet weirdly deadpan, with some quality of Buster Keaton, I think, if Keaton's character were allowed to use words. There is nothing in our literature like "Self-Portrait in a Convex Mirror," nothing like "The Skaters," or *Three Poems*. Ashbery provided a reintroduction into how a poem can sound, how it can think. Of course I never got Ashbery's voice out of my head. How could that happen? And, *pace* Bloom, one cannot even properly misread Ashbery; he provides space for his own misreadings, and so yours can fit only in the spaces he has already himself created!

And so I have loved Ashbery (and loved Koch, my teacher, and O'Hara, their friend; and, later, Schuyler too; and am still learning Shapiro, who just died, and Padgett). But there are aggravating things about Ashbery, especially in the later work, though the features were always there. He becomes ponderous, prescriptive; his use of "you" is tiresome. (Really, John, you *don't* mean me). His colloquialisms become boring. He becomes *cute*. He always had a talent for the expansive, but it started to become too much. He kept writing, but his style caricatured itself; I began to wonder if it had always been a caricature. There was always that risk.

And there was Ashbery's cult and all his imitators. And there was his personal aura, which I found kind of annoying. And then I'd see another of his poems in the *New York Review of Books*, and it would be dull, pretentious, and awful, like some AI Ashbery *avant la machine*. Like many poets with long lives, he wrote an enormous number of mediocre and even pretty bad poems. The great ones are what they are–and how many poets have come up with poems like those, and not a few of them?

Then he died. September 3, 2017. Everyone, it seemed, had something to say–most of it unambivalent praise, a lot of personal reminiscence. I had no personal reminiscence, and I am never unambivalent. But I felt I did have a response, for Ashbery's work, as I've said, was part of me. I did have an elegy of sorts to compose. But the only way I could feel to do it was to try to get inside his style: to evaluate through imitation; to parody.

So I wrote an Ode to Ashbery, in what at times veers into Ashbery's voice. An ode beside the ode. *Para-oidia*. Not the "anxiety"; perhaps the Hysterics of Influence. I open the Selected Poems at random:

All things seem mention of themselves
And the names which stem from them branch out to other referents.
Hugely, spring exists again. The weigela does its dusty thing
In fire-hammered air. And garbage trucks are heaved against
The railing... ["Grand Gallop," from *Self-Portrait*]

That's some good Ashbery. Can I ever write as well as that?

One risk of parody is that your writing just won't hold up to the original, and so the joke's on you.

7. Poetics/Politics/

I think that politics–the social-ethical value/meaning/being of poetry–is the fundamental question of poetics. The question is sometimes quite overt. In the Hebrew Bible, for instance, the verse sections of the prophets' writings clearly lay out ethical questions. Here's a well-known passage from Isaiah:

'Why, when we fasted, did You not see?
When we starved our bodies, did You pay no heed?'
Because on your fast day
You see to your business
And oppress all your laborers...
No, this is the fast I desire:
To unlock fetters of wickedness,
And untie the cords of the yoke,
To let the oppressed go free...
It is to share your bread with the hungry,
And to take the wretched into your home;
When you see the naked man, to clothe him,
And not to ignore your own kin   (58:3-7).

Plato thought that politics was the essential question regarding poetry. Beauty and dramatic tension were all well and good, according to Plato; his spokes-philosopher Socrates declared himself a great admirer of poets. But a just and well-ordered state required that all art be evaluated in terms of truthfulness and moral content. (Plato never read the Hebrew Bible, but if he had, I'm sure he'd have far more to object to than he found in Homer!). Later thinkers shared Plato's concerns, but came to different conclusions as to poetry's value. Phillip Sidney wittily stepped around the problem of truth, saying of the poet that "he nothing affirms, and therefore never lieth"! Sidney's wit is satisfying, but his thinking clearly needs to go further, for poetry obviously is fictive, is feigning–like all representation it stands in some relation to reality, and yet is not real. Even the claims of modernist and more recent art to a status of being objects in the world, as real as any other object, are both true and not true. Part of the status of being a piece of art is to exist in a history of the production and interpretation of art, such that we know that Cage's silence is music, that John's flags are paintings, and Rauschenburg's bed is part of a composition and is not meant to be slept in; Kenneth Goldsmith's transcriptions are poems–just extremely uninteresting ones. We--both the artists and the audiences--know these things, and cannot pretend that we don't. (Certainly since Arthur Danto's writing on art, we know). Works of art are indeed things that exist in the world, but they are very particular sorts of things; things that have meanings and the meanings necessarily have contexts and implications beyond any strictly "ontological" status. Works of art are social objects and our understandings, apprehensions, encounters of and with them have social meanings–and thus are political. This is obvious, I think. I can't think of what might be a cogent argument against some essentially political status for poetry.

I am not, however, thereby claiming that other social objects that are not art, or make no claims to being art, do not also have social meanings. This is obvious, I hope, and has been obvious since Roland Barthes' *Mythologies*, if not long before.

Nor am I claiming that all poems are political–either in some clearly evident way or in some more obscure, ideological sense. A poem about a garden can be read as indicating some set of class values and relations. Certainly. But there are also times when you read the poem about the garden and just really enjoy it as a poem about a garden. Why not? What seems to be the poem's intention (or the poet's) may be relevant to the reading, or may not. The poem may be naive, the poem may be disingenuous; the poem may also be beautiful. It may imagine a beautiful reconciliation of class antagonisms. This imagined reconciliation may be read as utopian, or it may be read as an evasion. It may be difficult to determine. The poem's beauty itself may constitute a utopian *promesse de bonheur*.

All this may be obvious.

And yet, I feel the need to rehearse this so that the obvious is also evident, for this is not always the case. ("Obvious" is a category of logic; "evident" is empirical).

Shelley spelled out what is still, I think, a basis for a political understanding of poetry. I don't refer primarily to the end of "A Defense of Poetry," the famous line about poets being "unacknowledged legislators of the world." That would be nice, but it's clearly a stretch. I mean more his argument against narrowly didactic poetry. The moral, and thus political, value of poetry is not that it tells you what is moral. Poetry's political value is that it "enlarges the circumference of the imagination," and imagination is "the great instrument of moral good." More specifically, Shelley asserts that this imaginative capacity opposes the general and pervasive ideology of "the calculating principle" that inevitably will "exacerbate at once the extremes of luxury and want… the Scylla and Charybdis of anarchy and despotism." Our knowledge and technical expertise, Shelley argues, is sufficient to create a just society with shared prosperity. What we lack is "the creative faculty to imagine that which we know; we want [that is, lack] the generous impulse to act that which we imagine; we want the poetry of life; our calculations have outrun conception." Poetry is unacknowledged legislation in the sense that its impulse is the liberated political will.

"OBU Manifesto #39"   (*The OBU Manifestos*)

If, returning to Shelley, poetry is that which "compels us to feel that which we perceive and to imagine that which we know"; if poetry "creates anew the universe, after it has been annihilated in our minds by the recurrence of impressions blunted by reiteration," then it must, on one hand defamiliarize our experience–and here Shelley very much anticipates Shklovsky– but it must, at the same time, be understood, or must move a reader somehow toward understanding. And so, OBU–One Big Union/Oligarchy Busters United (the Movement that Does Not Exist)–turns toward some passages from Whitman. That substance of greatest political urgency, OBU felt in those months following the election of 2016, was the effort to imagine and bring about some manner of solidarity. Not just "alliance," not just "intersection," but something stronger, more profound, more deeply human... some approximation of a "universal"!? There must be some utterance, some social vision that can be apprehended in common. We had entered a more intensive age of "enclosure." How could we rediscover the "common"?

Right, how?! Nothing could be agreed on. There was no shared terminology, no terminal toward which together we could point our political rails and trains. And yet, why not? Was there some neural capacity that simply wasn't there? Or were the regressive, poisonous ideologies of panic, cruelty, resentment, refusal of empathy simply too powerful to oppose effectively? Was Whitman's desperate, obdurate optimism simply a gross mistake? The manifesto begins with Whitman's common. By the end, it falls back to "the curved space of the untranslatable," to a hidden, circumscribed ethics of reading. Is that all we have? At last, we can only bring what we can bring.

Shelley's political poetics has much in common with his slightly older contemporary, Friedrich Schiller. (Shelley, I don't believe, ever read Schiller; Coleridge may have). Schiller also posited his ideas on the "aesthetic" in opposition to "utility...the great idol of the age" and against what he felt was "the spirit of the time, fluctuating between perverseness and brutality, between unnaturalness and mere Nature..." Early in his book *Letters Upon the Aesthetic Education of Man*, Schiller introduces a remarkable image for the attempt to reform a corrupt, unjust society while living within it. While a watch repairer must let the watch wind down and then repair it once its mechanism is stationary, "the living clockwork of the State must be repaired while it is in motion, and here it is a case of changing the wheels as they revolve" (29). How is this possible? It's a long shot, but Schiller's theory is one of play–a zone of free activity "in which sensuousness and reason are active at the same time" (98). Neither the senses nor reason by themselves can lead to a truly realized ethics and politics. One must posit some third, intermediate place that will bring humanity fully toward the ethical realm. In Schiller's theory, play and its cousin and offspring, art, are the only hopes for truly addressing an unjust social order–for repairing the social mechanism while it is in motion, as it always is.

And we're always in the midst of it. We can never reach an Archemedean point that will give us leverage to move things with certainty. As I wrote at the end of another poem included in this book, "...You're in it, you're of it, you're grasping/ at every detail as if a synecdoche were a life raft."

"Disintegrating Ode to a Senator"   (*The Obvious Poems and the Worthless Poems*)

Can you guess which Senator? That's right, it's Sen. Joe Manchin, the Coal Baron and Environmental Legislation Obstructor from West Virginia. Remember the absolute debacle of Manchin's derailing the climate bill in late 2021 and 2022?

It was around that time when I came up with the idea of a new movement for political redemption: The Unacknowledged Legislators: Poets for the Planet. OBU, of course, still did not exist and, by definition, could not exist. The UL was partly born through an agitation of Kent Johnson on FaceBook when he asked, What are the poets doing? What should they be doing–both as poets per se and as Poet-Citizens? What obligations are or should we be feeling, and then acting on? And so the Unacknowledged Legislators came into being, or non-being. Percy Shelley, President; myself as Recording Secretary; Kent Johnson, Social Director; Muriel Ruykeyser, Campaign Director.

I wrote some poems. Kent wrote some poems. Percy's and Muriel's poems were already written. And my book, *The Obvious Poems and the Worthless Poems* came about, as I mentioned in an earlier comment. The political poems are the obvious poems. What's there to say that hasn't been said and isn't utterly obvious? The poems of personal feeling and formal experiment are the worthless poems. Who cares what you say about your stupid life and so-called "poetics"?

There are forms in poetry and forms in nature. Forms indicate regularities, zones of relative predictability. Poetic forms' uses of repetition and variation build expectations and then, variously, fulfill or upend them. That's what form is, nothing else; glad we could get that settled. The world exhibits both regularities and change; but typically, over the course of human habitation on the planet, change has been gradual, generally undetectable over the course of an individual lifetime. Well, geological change can be sudden–earthquakes, volcanoes, and such. But the cycles of seasons have, since the last ice-age 10,000 years ago, been constant. And don't quibble, this is mostly true. Until now. So, I wrote a poem in which the disintegration of a poetic form stood as narrative and analogy for the disintegration of the presumed norms of climate. And the norms of civilized life as known for millennia are, as the poem conceives, dependent on the norms of climate. So.

I addressed the disintegrating ode to the Senator most responsible for abetting the disintegration. And then I wrote the following...

"and admit that the waters
  around you have grown..."
    –The Ancient Inundator
(*The Obvious Poems and the Worthless Poems*)

If the sea levels are rising, let the poetry levels rise as well. An absurd poem, for an absurd situation. (And the title is my only quotation, I should say, of a Nobel Prize winner!). My poems about our times in the abyss seem all to want to be funny. Why is this? Are these gestures toward humor a form of commentary on the poetics of a political poem? Am I saying that such poems are, in truth, impossible? Their intentions are entirely serious, but they cannot express themselves seriously. Perhaps the "Ode" sounds in earnest, yes; but it is close to humor. I am serious as a poet. I insist on the efficacy of poetry. I believe in Shelley and Schiller. I believe, with Marcuse in *The Aesthetic Dimension*, that "the need for radical change must be rooted in the subjectivity of individuals themselves, in their intelligence and their passions, their drives and their goals," and that a transformed subjectivity, person by person, can be "a counterforce" against the "aggressive and exploitative socialization" that characterizes our world. I believe that "the truth of art lies in its power to break the monopoly of established reality." I believe that art addresses "men and women capable of living in that community of freedom which is the potential of the species" and that "solidarity would be on weak grounds were it not rooted in the instinctual structures of individuals." I believe that art "aims at a new 'system of needs'," and that while art cannot change the world directly, it can "contribute to changing the consciousness and drives" of people who then will go on to change the world.

That's a lot to believe, and yet I believe it! That art can transform our "instinctual structures" and move us toward that great Marxian ideal of "species being"… of being, becoming, what we truly are and what we must become. Better. Better than what we are. The work of art, as with Rilke's "Archaic Torso," looks through you, through each thought and desire, each neuron, and atom, and you have no choice: *You must change your life*. Isn't it so?

But I don't believe it. It's complete nonsense.

"The only emperor is the emperor of ice cream."

The political poem, in my rendition, my poetics, inhabits both these vectors.

Flood the Capitol with poems, then. Look in your little mirror. Cause the ode to disintegrate, just as the world disintegrates, as if that analogy could possibly hold. I wish I could write a poem like this one of Rukeyser's:

I lived in the first century of world wars.
Most mornings I would be more or less insane,
The newspapers would arrive with their careless stories,
The news would pour out of various devices
Interrupted by attempts to sell products to the unseen.
I would call my friends on other devices;
They would be more or less mad for similar reasons.
Slowly I would get to pen and paper,
Make my poems for others unseen and unborn.
In the day I would be reminded of those men and women,
Brave, setting up signals across vast distances,
Considering a nameless way of living, of almost unimagined values.
As the lights darkened, as the lights of night brightened,
We would try to imagine them, try to find each other,
To construct peace, to make love, to reconcile
Waking with sleeping, ourselves with each other,

Ourselves with ourselves. We would try by any means
To reach the limits of ourselves, to reach beyond ourselves,
To let go the means, to wake.

I lived in the first century of these wars.

This is a poem I feel, but can't write.

"Addressing the Law"   (*The Obvious Poems and the Worthless Poems*)

This is the poem I *can* write. The echo of Kafka bouncing off of Shelley is intentional. Again, the poem is concerned with its form, and again the concern with form is something of a joke. I say how I tried to write political poems that would be *effective*, that would somehow blow a hole in the ship of Oligarchy, well, ok, would blow a *conceptual* hole in the ship and then, with luck, actual people would be inspired to take real actions toward justice and emancipation. The poem would elucidate our needed solidarities, our ethical obligations, the full and newly acknowledged legislation! But such a poem can only fail, and form is my retreat. "I want to play with stanzas." And, as any reader can see at a glance, the poem plays with stanzas. 3-line stanzas; 4-line stanzas; 5-line stanzas; then 4-line; 3-line; then 2-line. And the final, single line. "The world can go to hell." That was fun. The poem is a ripping apart of its own conceptions, playing out again the impasse of aesthetic play against the fiasco of moving social parts. "... and the time has come/ the time is now if time were something/ to be spoken of in any polite or sociable way..." But the only thing to be said about time is that we're wasting it, drowning it, burning it.

"OBU Manifesto #1,988"   (*The OBU Manifestos, vol. 2*)

This poem/manifesto gets to the critical point of where I don't know how to think. The text insists on the point that I keep insisting on: that a poem must be *read*, that "it means what it says," and whatever you might say *about* it is not what it is or means. A manifesto that attempts clearly to manifest what is not in the same order of manifestation may be of great interest, but it is not what it claims to be. At the same time, a poem can be written plainly so that it may establish some common space of understanding. Or it can be baffling, pointing in several directions, suggesting conjunction in some ways and evidently disjunctive in others–and there it is, like it or lump it.

I like writings on poetics that work like poems in this confluence of the common and the dislocating, and that may have a sense of humor regarding this interchange. How seriously do I have to take myself? Is everything really so clear as my theory appears to attest? I love Rachel's hybrid Midrashes in *The Pink Guitar*, her working to "change the instrument" that writes and understands poetry. I like a lot of Charles Bernstein's theoretical schtick–his "Recantorum" at the end of *Attack of the Dangerous Poems* is a wonderful piece of swiveling, absurdist poetics. What I don't like are essays in poetics that read like dogma. The writer has arrived at the privileged terminology that grants him or her the surest understanding of how poetry functions in its ideological context, and the writer understands as well exactly what is the social totality, how poetry or art are both products and contestations of that ideology, how, for instance, "the proliferation of signs and discourse is embedded in, limited in certain ways by, or collusive with, or inscribed in difference ways by: this outer horizon, this set of limits, this set of ideologies, this overall body of sense that makes language into an archive of social effects." This is Bruce Andrews in a 1985 essay published in *Poetics Journal*, reprinted in *A Guide to Poetics Journal* (ed. Hejinian and Watten, 2013). We see in much of the poetics of L=A=N=G=U=A=G=E writing a merging of Foucault, Saussure, Derrida, and Marx. Systems of power determine discourse; but discourse is unstable, its referents sliding; but discourse still is materially limiting as it is ideologically determined; that the cracking open of syntax, orthography, referentiality and semantics are counter-hegemonic acts; that correct theory can identify the contours of power, the illegitimacies of reference, the ideologies embedded in conventions of language…and with this knowledge comes the power to constitute uses of language that can at least abrade the transmissions of power embedded in language, if not smash those hegemonies completely.

Poetics of this sort make a claim to have achieved an Archimedean point; that is, a place outside the system, from which the theory can apply the leverage that will move the system. But as I see it, there is no Archimedean point, theoretical or anyhow. "Where are we? We're here. We're not there." It's the work, then, of imagination, of poetry itself, to fabricate some other place, and so then, "we are there. We are not here." What system? There is cruelty, there is oppression, theft, massacre, accumulation, empire; there are histories of violence, histories of hierarchy, and every document of civilization is a document of barbarism. But there are not, I don't think, the sorts of self-reflexive, forever mirroring closures and totalities of institutions conceived by Foucault and, differently, Debord. Forget Foucault. Restore Bakhtin and polyphony as more fruitful and accurate directions of theory. The struggles we're engaged in are in our languages, as elsewhere--against whatever prison-houses of language presume to impose themselves. To know the walls of a prison are the walls of a prison, you must have a vantage point outside the walls, to paraphrase Wittgenstein. And if you have that vantage point outside the walls, then you're not in the prison. But now I've contradicted myself. We're in, but we can see and imagine outside. We teleport, or lingua-port. That's what I was trying to say. It's not a prison or other "disciplinary institution" that we're in; it's something else.

It's what George Clooney said in *Oh Brother, Where Art Thou* when he and his escaped convict friends were trapped in a burning barn surrounded by police with machine guns. He said, "Boys, we're in a tight spot." I think that's where we are.

"I Once Met Kent Johnson"
(published in *I Once Met Kent Johnson: a Book of Tribute and Recognition*, edited by Mike Boughn and Billie Chernicoff)

I have no commentary to add to this. Kent–a great poet, forger, witness, translator and elucidator, gadfly and guerilla of poetry--died in 2022 at the age of 67.

8. Last Poems

"The nut stops here."   (*Prior*)

Without quite realizing it, I wrote the final poems of all my books as miniature summaries of the books' poetics. All are, in some measure, commentaries-transactions-enactments of generation, conception, transmission, procreation... of/in language; and, at the same time, documents of aporia. The poem is produced, and its production is imperative–by means of intention or by means of some other mechanism. And/or. "...infinity of ferns copulate to coal." "These vestibules"–i.e. these rooms, these stanzas– "repeat their ovulations." The socio-spiritual-lingual-psychologistics of the poem are as messy, liquid, and complexly coded as biology, and as prone to miscarriage and infertility.

"The child was there before,/ scalding the future."

"Manifesto# C#minor [approximately]"   (*The OBU Manifestos, vol. 2*)

More of OBUlation and Obgestation... but the distinctions have become too small to be heard, and anyway are drowned out by mocking laughter. The first book of OBU manifested a Utopian anger and humor and determination. The second revolves more around despair. OBU has been beatified, but now exists as some parodic version of St. Francis preaching in dissonances as the oligarchy persists.

This is actually not the final poem of *OBU vol.2*. It was my mistake; the final pages stuck together when I was checking, and I took this as the last poem, not seeing (and forgetting) that it was not. But I'm going to stay with my mistake for this book. The poem's silliness speaks to the overall sense of frustration and absurdity that fills the book. The actual final piece, "Manifesto #4,999," is more earnest and discursive. It's right; it's a good ending. It also contains some panic, but a calmer panic. So, I'll stick with the difficult micro-harmonies of St. OBU, the wound whose incision is so fine that it closes before the blood flows out.

"It has to be irregular"   (*The Obvious Poems and the Worthless Poems*)

The overwhelming, unmotivated (or surpassingly overmotivated) joy of formal creation. Plenitude: "no idea or feeling/ of compulsion// sudden abundance of thought/ for no reason." The poem unfolds according to its code, along its axes. But what code? What is "axial thought"? It arises out of itself– external form congruent with internal structure. A beautiful and whole vision of spontaneous, autonomous aesthetic (pro-)creation. This is the last of the "worthless" poems. Worthless in this world, in this age. But in some other? There's a line from Melville somewhere that I can't remember... might be some refiguring of the "through a glass darkly" bit in First Corinthians, but it's not coming to me. And there's Blake: "For there the babe is born in joy/ That was begotten in dire woe/ Just as we reap in joy the fruit/ That we with bitter tears did sow." ..... But even better! "The message/ is its action, result// as division, replica/ as cell sweet energy..." A form and method of mimesis that is frictionless and pure fruition.

Never, never to be. And yet, sometimes it feels that way.

"OBU Manifesto #42"   (*The OBU Manifestos*)

The poetics of not-poetry; of life? It does not make the point that one's life can be aestheticized or turned into art; that's not the point here, though it may be true in other contexts. The question is how to understand "the trudge." The trudge is what we are always engaged in and cannot give up until we die, or give up. It is the "quotidian," and there are many poetics of the quotidian. But this is not a poetics of the quotidian. The trudge may take notice of some "red wheel barrow" along the way, but not much depends on it. The trudge pertains to the difficult road toward some sort of solidarity– "both the vision and the journey toward the vision. The journey and the vision and the work are always intertwined. And the trudge is the twine."

There are Whitman-like lists in that long second paragraph. The trudge is stuff. The trudge is continual.

The trudge also explores the future. It is an "Inter-temporal Knowledge Drone" that brings back news of where we might want to go and of where we most definitely do not want to go– and the paths that lead to those places. Then we have to decide. This is the reverse of a poetics of pure fruition and plenitude. This is the poetics of the trudge, which will "congeal" "around each flash of truth."

And yet, also, it's not so different. The visions are linked; they contain each other. Both poems end as ongoing. There is the single line, "axial thought," that breaks the sequence of couplets and sends thought out into some distinct but undetermined direction. And the enigmatic last sentence of "Manifesto 42": "What we need to know, OBU suggests, is known... all but one thing." What's that one thing???

Figure it out.

"What I think is nothing"   (*Under the Impression*)
   ...a creature of would.

JAMES BERGER is now a Senior Lecturer in American Studies and English at Yale University, but he will retire after the Spring 2025 semester–after thirty years of university teaching and a prior ten years teaching in elementary schools. He is the author of two academic monographs: *After the End: Representations of Post-Apocalypse* (U. of Minnesota Press, 1999) and *The Disarticulate: Language, Disability, and the Narratives of Modernity* (NYU Press, 2014); and of three books of poetry: *Prior* (BlazeVox, 2013), *Under the Impression* (BlazeVox, 2020), and *The Obvious Poems and the Worthless Poems* (Spuyten Duyvil, 2023). He is also midwife and conduit of *The OBU Manifestos, vols 1&2* (Dispatches Editions/Spuyten Duyvil, 2017, 2019).

He is currently at work on two books: "On Naive and Sentimental Poetics" and "The Book of Impasses." He will not tell you what genres these books might occupy.

www.ingramcontent.com/pod-product-compliance
Lightning Source LLC
LaVergne TN
LVHW060135080526
838202LV00050B/4120